THE ULTIMATE
POLICE TRAINER'S
PLAYBOOK

THE ULTIMATE
POLICE TRAINER'S
PLAYBOOK

Mastering Impactful Openers and Lasting Closers in Training

Antonio Zarzoza, "Instructor Z"

PALMETTO
PUBLISHING
Charleston, SC
www.PalmettoPublishing.com

Copyright © 2024 by Antonio Zarzoza, "Instructor Z."

All rights reserved
No portion of this book may be reproduced, stored in a retrieval system, or transmitted in any form by any means–electronic, mechanical, photocopy, recording, or other–except for brief quotations in printed reviews, without prior permission of the author.

Hardcover ISBN: 9798822967502
Paperback ISBN: 9798822966833

Figure 1: Instructor Z speaking at the 2023 TCOLE Conference

S.T.A.R.T. strong and E.N.D.I.T. stronger with Instructor Z.

TABLE OF CONTENTS

FOREWORD i
PROLOGUE v
INTRODUCTION: TRANSFORMING TRAINING WITH THE
ULTIMATE POLICE TRAINER'S PLAYBOOK vii

CHAPTER 1: FIRST IMPRESSIONS AND LASTING IMPACT—
       THE FLIGHT ANALOGY 1
CHAPTER 2: S.T.A.R.T. FRAMEWORK OVERVIEW 7
CHAPTER 3: STORY—ENGAGE AND CONNECT 13

**INSTRUCTOR Z's PRO TIP: ELEVATING YOUR
PRESENTATIONS WITH IVS** 20

CHAPTER 4: TESTIMONIAL—BUILDING TRUST 23
CHAPTER 5: ANALOGY—SIMPLIFYING COMPLEX CONCEPTS . 29
CHAPTER 6: RHETORICAL QUESTION—SPARKING
       REFLECTION 35
CHAPTER 7: TAKEAWAY—SETTING LEARNING
       EXPECTATIONS 39

**INSTRUCTOR Z's PRO TIP: S.T.A.R.T. YOUR OPENER WITH
FLEXIBILITY** 44

CHAPTER 8: TEACHING BY DESIGN VS. TEACHING BY
       DEFAULT 47
CHAPTER 9: SLIDE DESIGN VS. SLIDE DECORATION—
       CRAFTING VISUAL SYMPHONIES 53

**INSTRUCTOR Z's PRO TIP: UNLOCKING THE POWER OF
PURPOSEFUL SLIDE DESIGN** 58

CHAPTER 10: THE POWER OF PERSUASION—LEVERAGING ETHOS, PATHOS, AND LOGOS IN YOUR OPENERS AND CLOSERS 63
CHAPTER 11: THE SIX LAWS OF LEARNING—YOUR FOUNDATION FOR S.T.A.R.T. AND E.N.D.I.T. 69
CHAPTER 12: NAILING THE CLOSER WITH E.N.D.I.T.—FRAMEWORK OVERVIEW. 75
CHAPTER 13: ENSURE NO QUESTIONS REMAIN 81
CHAPTER 14: NAIL DOWN KEY TAKEAWAYS. 85
CHAPTER 15: DRIVE ACTION. 91
CHAPTER 16: INSPIRE WITH AN EVOCATIVE STATEMENT 97
CHAPTER 17: TIE IT ALL TOGETHER WITH A CLEAR CLOSER. 103

INSTRUCTOR Z's PRO TIP: THE ESSENTIAL DIFFERENCE BETWEEN S.T.A.R.T. AND E.N.D.I.T. 108

CHAPTER 18: S.T.A.R.T. TO E.N.D.I.T.—A SEAMLESS LEARNING EXPERIENCE 111
CHAPTER 19: ADVANCED STRATEGIES FOR TEACHING EXCELLENCE 115
CHAPTER 20: ELEVATE AND EMPOWER—THE FINAL TAKEAWAY. 121

ACKNOWLEDGMENTS 123
REFERENCES 125
ABOUT THE AUTHOR 129

DEDICATION

To those who step up with a genuine passion to inspire, win hearts, and transform minds in the relentless pursuit of excellence.

To all who have entrusted me with their journey, believing not just in what I wholeheartedly share with them but also in the care and dedication I hold for the growth of others.

This is for you—the ones who dare to make a difference every single time.

—Z

Figure 2: Some of the many instructors I've had the pleasure of training—this book is for all of you

FOREWORD

How often have you been sitting in a class, wondering why you need to be there while thinking about the stockpile of different things you have waiting for your attention? The instructor walks to the front of the classroom and advances the presentation to a single slide with a wordy biography of their experience and accomplishments. They then advance to a bullet-point list of the performance objectives they intend for you to meet by the end of class. At this point, you've looked at the clock at least a dozen times, and it seems like time is going backward as you are thinking, "Why am I here?"

If an instructor doesn't capture the audience's attention in the first few minutes of class, it exponentially increases the difficulty of ever getting their attention. Even if the material is amazing, they are fighting a constant battle to gain student engagement. Trainers need to affect students' emotions before they can affect their knowledge and skills. In *The Ultimate Police Trainer's Playbook: Mastering Impactful Openers and Lasting Closers in Training*, Antonio Zarzoza, known to most as "Instructor Z," will help you intentionally craft your classes to seize the audience's attention and get them actively engaged from the start.

Then there's this scenario: You attended a good class with an instructor who was passionate about the topic. The presentation kept your attention, and the material was solid. But at the end of class, the instructor had no idea how to wrap it up and was as clumsy as a teenager on a first date. The ending just left you wanting more. Instead of leaving class satisfied, you leave wondering what to do with the information you learned, or worse, questioning whether it was applicable to you.

Instructors need to capture the audience's attention, keep them engaged throughout class, and finish with an ending they can't forget. Much like a great movie, teachers want to get the audience engaged, keep them listening with rapt attention, and give them a conclusion that wraps up the class with a sense of resolution and emotional fulfillment. A visually striking ending—using powerful imagery or symbolism and uplifting or impactful music—should reinforce the message of the class and enhance the emotional impact created by the powerful opening. Finally, trainers should challenge their students with a call to action. This is essential for encouraging accountability and empowering them to turn inspiration into tangible results.

I first met Instructor Z during an International Law Enforcement Educators and Trainers Association (ILEETA) Conference & Expo in St. Louis, Missouri, where he presented a class called "PowerPoint Design with Cinematics." As someone who is less than interested in computers or technology in general, I knew my presentations left room for improvement when it came to how I utilized PowerPoint. To say I was blown away by his class is an understatement. The material he presented was terrific, and I was able to apply many of the concepts from class. However, what made a lasting impression was how he managed the class from beginning to end.

Even if you've never had the pleasure of attending a class taught by Instructor Z, a quick internet and social media search will provide you with numerous examples of why his classes are well-attended and the topic of conversation weeks, months, and sometimes years afterward.

He masterfully sets the stage and creates a bold and indelible impact before he utters a single word. He captures your attention and holds it throughout the class. At the end, he summarizes everything and leaves you ready to hit the ground running, eager to apply the new information. Instructor Z is, quite simply, one of the best and most talented instructors anywhere.

Instructors and trainers who adopt and utilize his S.T.A.R.T. and E.N.D.I.T. frameworks, as outlined in Instructor Z's *The Ultimate Police Trainer's Playbook: Mastering Impactful Openers and Lasting Closers in Training*, will find more audience engagement, a greater degree of influence on their students, and a lasting example of what an outstanding instructor does to connect with their students. Instructor Z shares a simple-to-use methodology for creating meaningful, memorable, and engaging presentations.

If you had a chance to become the next Instructor Z, why wouldn't you take the opportunity? *The Ultimate Police Trainer's Playbook: Mastering Impactful Openers and Lasting Closers in Training* is every trainer's opportunity to improve their presentations and create lasting learning experiences. As trainers, we owe it to our students to be better. This book will give you the tools to make a lasting impact on your learners. I challenge you to apply the S.T.A.R.T. framework for impactful beginnings and the E.N.D.I.T. framework for purposeful conclusions. Just like Instructor Z, I urge you to use these principles to teach not by default but by intentional design.

Todd Fletcher
Combative Firearms Training, LLC

PROLOGUE

Imagine you are about to take off on a flight. As the engines roar and the plane accelerates, those first moments in the air set the tone for everything that follows. A smooth ascent puts everyone at ease, and even though turbulence may lie ahead, you are confident that the pilot knows exactly what they are doing. Now, think about the landing. When the plane begins its descent, you want it to be precise and steady. You do not want to feel rushed, uncertain, or wondering if the landing gear will engage.

Training sessions are no different. The moment you step into the room or start your presentation, your audience is forming first impressions. They are subconsciously asking, "What's in it for me?" (WIIFM) and deciding if you are worth their time. In those critical first moments, you either captivate their attention or risk losing them to the distractions of everyday life. Just like a smooth flight, how you end matters just as much. A rushed or weak closing leaves your participants disengaged, and the impact of your message fizzles away.

This book, *The Ultimate Police Trainer's Playbook: Mastering Impactful Openers and Lasting Closers in Training*, is your guide to transforming your training sessions by mastering the art of impactful starts and powerful finishes. It is about creating experiences with intentional design, where every word, story, and action paves the way for successful learning.

The frameworks within—crafted through years of experience and countless workshops—will help you set the stage for meaningful engagement and ensure your audience leaves with lasting, memorable takeaways.

But let us make one thing clear: this is not a quick fix for dull presentations. It is about teaching by design, not by default. You will learn how to elevate your training from the ordinary to the extraordinary, not by following some rigid formula but by crafting moments of genuine impact. The goal is not just to *teach*—it is to inspire, engage, and transform.

As you start this journey, ask yourself: *What would happen if every class I taught opened with purpose and closed with power?* The answers await you. So let us begin this journey toward mastery.

Welcome to *The Ultimate Police Trainer's Playbook*.

—Z

INTRODUCTION
TRANSFORMING TRAINING WITH THE ULTIMATE POLICE TRAINER'S PLAYBOOK

In training, as in life, how you begin and how you end can make all the difference. Whether you are guiding seasoned professionals or new recruits, your ability to connect with learners from the first moment to the last is key to a successful session. But how can you ensure that your training doesn't just start well but also leaves a lasting, meaningful impact? This is where *The Ultimate Police Trainer's Playbook* comes into play.

This book offers you a blueprint for creating training sessions that capture attention right from the outset and conclude with a powerful closing, ensuring that the learning experience sticks long after the session ends. The key to impactful training delivery lies in both your first and last impressions. These moments are not random or accidental; they are crafted with intention, conscious effort, and deliberate design. When you approach your training with purpose, you elevate the entire experience for your learners.

RELEVANCE IS KEY: THE WIIFM PRINCIPLE

At the core of any effective training is the concept of relevance. Adult learners need to understand immediately why they should invest their time and energy in your session. This is where the **WIIFM principle**—*What's In It For Me?*—comes into play. From the moment they sit down, learners are subconsciously asking themselves how the material will benefit them.

Research in adult learning supports this. According to Malcolm Knowles' principles of andragogy, adults are more motivated to learn when they understand how the material applies directly to their personal or professional lives. They need to know the "why" before they are willing to engage with the "how" and the "what." This is why your training must be purposeful right from the start, answering the WIIFM question in the opening moments. By doing so, you set the stage for an engaged and invested audience, primed to absorb and retain what you present.

Your ability to consciously address WIIFM at the beginning of your session is essential. If you cannot connect the material to the learners' needs early on, you risk losing their attention. When you create a session opener that is both deliberate and relevant, you are doing more than capturing attention—you are fostering an environment where learners see immediate value in what is to come. This is the first step toward delivering a training experience that sticks.

THE PLAYBOOK: S.T.A.R.T. AND E.N.D.I.T.

The **S.T.A.R.T.** and **E.N.D.I.T.** frameworks provide a structured, purposeful approach to beginning and ending your training sessions. With **S.T.A.R.T.**, you will learn how to craft openers that draw learners in using **Stories**, **Testimonials**, **Analogies**, **Rhetorical Question**, and

Takeaways. These elements help you establish relevance and connect with your audience right from the start. When you open with intention, using these strategies consciously, you are not just delivering content—you are creating an experience.

For example:

- **Story (S)**: Humanize the content with a story that resonates and makes the material relatable.
- **Testimonial (T)**: Validate the material's importance with real-life examples.
- **Analogy (A)**: Clarify complex ideas by comparing them to familiar situations.
- **Rhetorical Question (R)**: Spark curiosity with questions that challenge learners to think critically.
- **Takeaway (T)**: Establish early on what learners can expect to gain, providing a clear benefit from the start.

When used with deliberate intent, each of these elements helps you not only engage your learners but also establish a meaningful connection to the material. By the end of this book, you will see how these small but powerful tools, when used intentionally, lead to greater engagement and retention.

At the other end of the session, **E.N.D.I.T.** ensures that your training leaves a lasting impression. Using the **Ensure no questions remain, Nail down key takeaways, Drive action, Inspire with a statement**, and **Tie it all together** approach, you will conclude your session with impact. The closing moments are your last chance to reinforce the material and inspire learners to apply what they have learned. Much like the opener, your closer must be purposeful and crafted with a conscious effort to leave a lasting impact.

FIRST AND LAST IMPRESSIONS: MORE THAN JUST BOOKENDS

While first and last impressions are the anchors of a session, they are part of a much larger whole. The **primacy** and **recency effects**—two well-established principles in psychology—show that people tend to remember what they learn first and last most clearly. By making the most of these moments, you maximize retention. But the S.T.A.R.T. and E.N.D.I.T. frameworks are not just about making your training bookends memorable; they are about making the entire session flow smoothly and purposefully.

First and last impressions help learners make sense of everything that happens in between. When you open strong and end with a clear, impactful message, the middle of your session—the core of your content—becomes easier for learners to digest. This approach allows you to structure your training in a way that is both intentional and effective, ensuring that learners leave with the knowledge and tools they need.

YOUR PLAYBOOK FOR TRANSFORMATIVE TRAINING

This book is designed to give you actionable strategies that you can apply to any training session. Whether you are preparing a workshop, lecture, or presentation, the S.T.A.R.T. and E.N.D.I.T. frameworks will guide you in creating an experience that is impactful, purposeful, and transformative. By integrating these frameworks into your delivery, you will learn to:

- Craft openers that capture attention and establish relevance.
- Create closers that reinforce key takeaways and inspire action.
- Engage your learners throughout the session with deliberate techniques.

- Use psychological principles to improve retention and comprehension.

With *The Ultimate Police Trainer's Playbook* in hand, you will be equipped to take your training to the next level. You will move beyond generic presentations and create sessions that connect with your audience on a deeper level—sessions that are both impactful and with a lasting experience. Through intentional design and conscious effort, you will not just deliver content; you will deliver transformation.

CHAPTER 1
FIRST IMPRESSIONS AND LASTING IMPACT—THE FLIGHT ANALOGY

"Well begun, is half done."
—Aristotle

In any learning environment, first and last impressions are critical. Think of a classroom session as a flight. The takeoff sets the tone for the journey, and the landing determines how the entire experience will be remembered. Just like a shaky takeoff can leave passengers unsettled, a poorly executed opener in training can disengage learners right from the start. Similarly, a rough landing—or a rushed, uninspired conclusion—leaves students walking away without the lasting impact you intended.

In *The Ultimate Police Trainer's Playbook: Mastering Impactful Openers and Lasting Closers in Training*, we explore the science behind these critical moments. The *primacy and recency effects*—cognitive principles that explain how people remember the first and last elements of a sequence more than the middle—support the importance of creating strong, impactful openers and lasting closers (Murdock, 1962). For trainers, mastering these moments can transform a session from a forgettable lecture into a learning experience that resonates long after the class ends.

THE POWER OF A STRONG TAKEOFF (THE OPENER)

The beginning of any training session is where you capture attention and build rapport with your learners. If you fumble this moment, like a bumpy takeoff, the entire session may suffer from disengaged learners. Research shows that capturing attention early is crucial, as student motivation and engagement are often highest at the start (Guthrie & Wigfield, 2000). Failing to make a strong impression during the opening can cause students to disengage, making it much harder to regain their focus.

The secret to a strong opener lies in addressing the unspoken question on every learner's mind: *What's in it for me?* (WIIFM). People are naturally more inclined to invest their attention when they see a direct benefit to themselves. Whether you open with a provocative question, a relevant story, or a surprising fact, the key is to show learners why they should care about what is coming next. By making this connection early on, you create a learning environment that invites curiosity and participation.

MASTERING THE MID-FLIGHT: KEEPING ENGAGEMENT HIGH

Once the session is underway, maintaining the learners' attention is critical. This is the "cruising altitude" of the lesson, where the trainer might feel comfortable, but complacency here can derail the entire experience. Effective trainers continuously monitor engagement and adjust as necessary to keep learners interested.

The tools we use—whether PowerPoint, Google Slides, Prezi, or Canva—are integral to this process. But these tools alone will not ensure engagement. In fact, research published in the *Journal of Educational Psychology* emphasizes that multimedia presentations can enhance retention, but only when used thoughtfully to complement the teaching, not replace it (Mayer, 2002).

This is where we see the common pitfalls of *Death by PowerPoint* (or Prezi or Canva). A presentation overloaded with text, irrelevant images, or excessive animations can detract from learning rather than enhance it. When slides are cluttered or poorly designed, they often serve as a crutch for the instructor, leading to *PowerPoint Karaoke*—a scenario where the trainer reads directly from the slides, turning their back to the audience and disengaging from the learners. This approach not only weakens the delivery but also creates a passive learning environment where students tune out (Alley et al., 2006).

To avoid this, slides should be student-centered, visually engaging, and relevant to the key points being discussed. They must enhance, not overwhelm, the content. Minimalist design—focusing on clear, essential information and visuals that reinforce learning—has been shown to increase engagement and retention (Sweller, 1988). Effective trainers know that the goal of a presentation is not to impress with flashy slides but to facilitate understanding and connection with the material.

AVOIDING POWERPOINT KARAOKE: THE DEATH OF ENGAGEMENT

One of the greatest pitfalls of modern presentations is the overreliance on slides as scripts. Too often, instructors use slides as teleprompters, reading word-for-word from the screen while disengaging from their audience. This so-called "phenomenon," sarcastically known as PowerPoint Karaoke, diminishes the effectiveness of the lesson and causes learners to lose interest. A study in the *Journal of Business and Technical Communication* confirmed that students are significantly less engaged when instructors read from slides, reducing both interaction and content retention (Alley et al., 2006).

Instead of allowing slides to dominate the lesson, they should function as visual aids that support and enhance the narrative. Eye contact, movement, and interaction with students are critical for maintaining engagement. The trainer should always be the focal point, using the slides to reinforce the message, not to deliver it.

AIMING HIGHER: CREATING RESONANCE BEYOND THE CLASSROOM

Great trainers aim to leave a lasting impact. Your responsibility does not end when the lesson is over. The real success of a training session is measured by how much of it resonates with learners long after they leave the room. Adult learning theory emphasizes the importance of applying knowledge to real-world scenarios, which means the lesson must connect with the learners' lives and experiences (Knowles, 1980). Your goal should be to craft lessons that leave an imprint on their minds, driving them to think critically and apply what they have learned.

Instructors who focus only on delivering content in the classroom miss this crucial opportunity. *The Ultimate Police Trainer's Playbook* urges trainers to design sessions that transcend the immediate moment, creating learning experiences that remain relevant long after the session concludes. To achieve this, lessons must be engaging, memorable, and applicable. This requires intention—not only in delivery but also in the design of the visual aids, the flow of the session, and the way you connect key points to the learners' personal and professional contexts.

THE IMPORTANCE OF A SMOOTH LANDING (THE CLOSER)

Just like a flight, a lesson's ending can determine the entire experience's impact. A rushed or disengaged closer can undermine even the most well-crafted content. Research on the *recency effect* indicates that people remember the final moments of an experience more vividly than the middle, making the closing of a session an essential moment for reinforcing key takeaways (Ebbinghaus, 1885).

In your closer, it is vital to summarize the key points, tie everything back to the learning objectives, and leave learners with a clear sense of how they can apply what they have learned. A strong closer not only ensures that students walk away with clarity but also inspires them to act. When done right, the closing becomes the most powerful part of the lesson, cementing the learning experience and encouraging application beyond the classroom.

Figure 3: Keep your audience engaged and connect with them

In *The Ultimate Police Trainer's Playbook: Mastering Impactful Openers and Lasting Closers in Training*, we emphasize that the most effective trainers are those who understand the importance of every phase of the learning journey—from the first impression to the final takeaway. By mastering the opener, maintaining engagement through thoughtful design and delivery, and finishing strong with a memorable and lasting closer, trainers can elevate their sessions into transformative experiences. It is about more than just delivering content; it is about crafting lessons that resonate, inspire, and leave a lasting impact.

CHAPTER 2
S.T.A.R.T. FRAMEWORK OVERVIEW

> *"Start strong, stay strong, and finish strong by remembering why you started in the first place."*
> —Ralph Marston

In *The Ultimate Police Trainer's Playbook: Mastering Impactful Openers and Lasting Closers in Training*, one of the most powerful tools to deliver an impactful and engaging training session is the S.T.A.R.T. framework. This system, which I developed through years of research, experience, and reflection, is rooted in evidence-based learning principles but refined to meet the practical needs of trainers across various fields. The framework's purpose is simple: ensure that your presentations not only capture your audience's attention but also leave a lasting impression that drives real-world application.

The S.T.A.R.T. framework comprises five core elements: **Story, Testimonial, Analogy, Rhetorical Question**, and **Takeaway**. Each of these elements is designed to foster engagement and enhance retention by creating an emotional and intellectual connection between the material and the audience. While these components are grounded in long-standing educational theories, they have been refined into a proven system that has transformed both my presentations and the teaching of countless instructors I have mentored.

1. Story

- **Purpose:** To create an emotional connection that draws the audience into the content, making abstract ideas more tangible and relatable.

Stories are one of the most effective tools for engaging learners because they activate both emotional and cognitive pathways in the brain. Research shows that storytelling can boost memory retention by linking facts with emotions (Graesser, Olde, & Klettke, 2002). By setting up a narrative, you give learners a context they can relate to, making the material feel relevant and memorable (Green & Brock, 2000).

Example: *In my crisis intervention training, I often begin with a story about a veteran officer dealing with a mental health crisis. This scenario immediately connects emotionally with participants who have faced similar situations. By introducing the topic through a story, I grab the audience's attention and prepare them for the deeper, strategy-based content that follows.*

2. Testimonial

- **Purpose:** To provide credible reinforcement of the content by sharing real-world validation, establishing trust and confidence in the material.

Testimonials offer a form of social proof that reinforces the relevance and credibility of your teaching. Studies in social psychology highlight that hearing about others' successes increases our confidence in applying new information.

Example: *In my Ethical Warrior Seminar, I begin by sharing a quote from Thomas Jefferson: "In matters of style, swim with the flow; in matters of principle, stand like a rock." This quote sets the tone for the entire seminar by encouraging officers to be adaptable in areas like technology and uniform standards but unyielding in their core values, such as integrity and fairness. This testimonial from history not only lends credibility to the lesson but also resonates deeply with officers who are often navigating the tension between evolving practices and unchanging principles.*

3. Analogy

- **Purpose:** To simplify complex concepts by comparing them to familiar, relatable experiences, making the content easier to grasp.

Analogies help bridge the gap between abstract ideas and practical understanding. According to research in educational psychology, analogical reasoning is a powerful tool for enhancing comprehension, especially when learners encounter new or difficult concepts.

Example: *In my Bulletproof Command Presence class, I use the analogy of two paintings: one, a rough sketch done with scribbles, and the other, a masterpiece of remarkable detail and impact. I ask the audience, "What does the world see when they look at you in uniform? A mere sketch of a police officer or the masterpiece of a professional law enforcement officer?" This analogy makes the abstract concept of "command presence" more accessible by helping officers visualize the importance of how they present themselves and how others perceive them.*

4. Rhetorical Question

- **Purpose:** To encourage critical thinking and self-reflection, prompting learners to engage with the material on a deeper, personal level.

Rhetorical questions are powerful because they stimulate internal dialogue without requiring an immediate response. Educational theorists have long noted that self-questioning encourages learners to think critically and engage more deeply with the material.

Example: *In my Master Police Instructor course, I ask, "Are you teaching by default, or are you teaching by design?" This rhetorical question encourages instructors to reflect on their own teaching styles. It pushes them to think about whether they are merely going through the motions or actively shaping meaningful learning experiences for their students. This moment of reflection sets the stage for discussing the importance of intentional instructional design.*

5. Takeaway

- **Purpose:** To provide a clear, actionable conclusion that reinforces the key lessons and encourages immediate application of the material.

Takeaways are essential for ensuring that learners leave with practical, applicable insights. Cognitive science tells us that learners need clear, concise conclusions to solidify what they have learned and integrate it into their work.

Example: *In my PowerPoint Design with Cinematics workshop, I conclude with this takeaway: "We will blur the lines between the magic of cinema and* the canvas of *PowerPoint*, mastering advanced yet simple design techniques to elevate slides into visually engaging works of art." This statement encapsulates the key goals of the workshop, motivating participants to see *PowerPoint* not as a simple presentation tool but as a creative platform capable of captivating an audience. By framing the takeaway this way, I inspire participants to apply what they have learned in innovative ways.

Conclusion

The S.T.A.R.T. framework is more than a collection of strategies: it is a comprehensive system grounded in proven learning techniques and years of practical experience. Each element—Story, Testimonial, Analogy, Rhetorical Question, and Takeaway—plays a critical role in helping instructors engage learners on both an emotional and intellectual level. This framework has been transformative, not only in my own presentations but also for the many trainers who have entrusted me with their development.

By implementing the S.T.A.R.T. framework as outlined in *The Ultimate Police Trainer's Playbook: Mastering Impactful Openers and Lasting Closers in Training*, you will see the impact it has on your teaching. It will help you create presentations that resonate with your learners, engage their minds, and leave lasting impressions, setting you apart as a truly engaging instructor.

CHAPTER 3
STORY—ENGAGE AND CONNECT

> *"Storytelling is the most powerful way to put ideas into the world today."*
> —Robert McKee

Storytelling has been one of the most powerful tools for communication and learning throughout history. From ancient oral traditions to modern training environments, stories have always served to connect people, transmit knowledge, and create shared experiences. In *The Ultimate Police Trainer's Playbook: Mastering Impactful Openers and Lasting Closers in Training*, storytelling takes on a significant role in helping instructors craft impactful training sessions. This chapter explores the psychological power of storytelling, its key elements, and the value of using stories as class openers, particularly with the S.T.A.R.T. framework. We will also provide exercises to help instructors refine their storytelling abilities and apply them effectively in their training.

THE PSYCHOLOGICAL POWER OF STORYTELLING IN TRAINING

Humans are naturally wired to respond to stories. When we hear a story, multiple areas of the brain are activated, engaging regions responsible for language processing, emotion, and even sensory experiences (Haven, 2007). This means that stories can help learners absorb and remember information better than raw data or lectures alone. By using stories in training, instructors can make abstract concepts more relatable and concrete, allowing learners to engage with the material on both an intellectual and emotional level.

In high-stakes professions like law enforcement, corrections, and emergency services, storytelling is particularly effective. For example, sharing a story about a difficult decision made during a critical incident helps trainees visualize themselves in that situation. According to research by Paul Zak, stories stimulate the release of oxytocin, a neurochemical linked to empathy and trust, fostering emotional engagement and making lessons more memorable (Zak, 2014).

Through storytelling, instructors can go beyond merely conveying information. They can build a connection with their learners, foster emotional investment, and create lasting impressions that translate into real-world skills.

THE VALUE OF USING A STORY AS AN OPENER WITH THE S.T.A.R.T. FRAMEWORK

Many trainers begin their sessions with a standard introduction: "Good morning, my name is…" or "Today we'll be covering…" While this approach may serve its purpose, it often fails to engage learners from the outset. It sets the tone for a session that feels routine, predictable, and uninspired.

Using a **story as an opener**—particularly with the **S.T.A.R.T. framework** (Story, Testimonial, Analogy, Rhetorical Question, Takeaway)—transforms the opening moments of a training session into something more captivating and emotionally impactful. A well-told story grabs attention, draws learners in, and gives them a reason to care about what comes next. It sets the stage for a session that is not just informative but also engaging and transformative.

WHY A STORY HOOKS THE AUDIENCE

Starting a session with a compelling story hooks the audience in ways that no traditional introduction can. A story immediately evokes curiosity, empathy, and emotional engagement. According to research by Kendall Haven, stories activate the brain's release of dopamine, which is linked to motivation and attention (Haven, 2007). This emotional and neurological engagement ensures that learners are more invested from the start, making them open to learning and retaining the information that follows.

For example, in police leadership training, instead of opening with a dry definition of leadership, an instructor could begin by sharing a story about an officer stepping up in a crisis. The tension, conflict, and eventual resolution in that story invite the learners to place themselves in that scenario and ask themselves how they would respond. By the time the story concludes, learners are emotionally connected to the material and ready to engage.

PREPPING THE AUDIENCE FOR A DISRUPTIVE AND IMPACTFUL EXPERIENCE

Using a story at the beginning of a session also sets the expectation that the training will be different—compelling, thought-provoking, and memorable. It signals to learners that this will not be the "typical class" but rather a session that challenges them to think, feel, and actively participate.

The **S.T.A.R.T. framework** helps trainers craft openers that serve this purpose:

- **Story**: A compelling narrative that draws learners into the material from the start.
- **Testimonial**: A real-life account that adds credibility and emotional weight to the lesson.
- **Analogy**: A comparison that simplifies complex concepts, making them easier to understand.
- **Rhetorical Question**: A thought-provoking question that encourages learners to reflect and engage with the material.
- **Takeaway**: A clear message that leaves learners with something meaningful to consider as the session progresses.

This approach contrasts sharply with the traditional "greeting and agenda" method. When a session begins with a captivating story or analogy, it primes learners for active engagement, not passive listening. It opens the door for a session that is not only informative but also energizing, leaving a lasting impact on the audience.

THE ELEMENTS OF A COMPELLING STORY

Although storytelling is a universal human experience, crafting an effective story for training requires attention to several key elements. A well-constructed story is more than just an anecdote—it is a structured narrative that teaches, challenges, and inspires action.

1. **Character**: Every story needs a central character. This is the person through whom the audience experiences the narrative. In training, this character might be the instructor sharing a personal experience or a fictional figure representing the learners. The character must be relatable so that learners can see themselves in the story.

2. **Setting**: The setting provides context for the story. It places the audience in a specific time and place, helping them visualize the scenario. Whether it is a tense moment on a dark street or a high-stakes decision in a courtroom, the setting grounds the story in reality.

3. **Conflict**: Conflict is the heart of any story. It is the challenge or problem the character must overcome. Without conflict, there is no tension, and without tension, there is no engagement. In training, conflict can take many forms—ethical dilemmas, critical decisions, or high-pressure situations. Presenting conflict invites learners to think critically and consider how they would handle the situation.

4. **Resolution**: Every story needs a resolution. This is where the conflict is addressed or solved. In training, the resolution should tie directly into the lesson's objectives, showing the importance of specific behaviors or decisions.

5. **Takeaway**: The takeaway is the moral or lesson of the story. This is the key message the instructor wants the learners to remember. In training, it is important that the takeaway aligns with the learning objectives, ensuring the story serves a clear educational purpose.

WHY STORIES WORK ACROSS PROFESSIONS

Storytelling's effectiveness is not limited to law enforcement or emergency services. It is a tool that works across disciplines because it taps into universal human emotions and experiences. Whether in healthcare, business, or education, stories help make abstract concepts more concrete and relatable.

In healthcare, for example, patient narratives help medical professionals connect emotionally with the ethical and practical challenges of their work. In business, stories of overcoming adversity or managing conflict teach leadership and resilience. Stephen Denning, an expert on storytelling in leadership, argues that stories allow people to feel the message, creating a stronger emotional connection (Denning, 2011).

The power of storytelling lies in its ability to bridge the gap between theory and practice. By using stories, trainers in any field can bring abstract ideas to life, making them more relatable and easier to apply in the real world.

EXERCISES AND REFLECTIONS FOR DEVELOPING STORYTELLING SKILLS

Exercise 1: Identify Personal Stories

- **Objective**: Develop a list of three personal or professional stories that could be used in a training context.
- **Instructions**: Write a brief outline of each story, including the character, setting, conflict, resolution, and takeaway. Share one of these stories with a colleague or peer and ask for feedback on how engaging and relevant it feels for your target audience.

Exercise 2: Story Adaptation

- **Objective**: Adapt a story for different audiences.
- **Instructions**: Take a single story and adapt it for three diverse types of learners—new recruits, experienced professionals, and leaders. Consider how you would alter the conflict, resolution, or takeaway for each group.

Reflection 1: Emotional Engagement

- **Question**: Reflect on a story that deeply moved you, either personally or professionally. What elements of the story were most impactful? How did it influence your thinking or behavior?

Reflection 2: Storytelling Beyond Your Field

- **Question**: Think of a story from another profession or field that taught you something valuable. How did it apply to your work, and what lessons did you take from it?

Conclusion: The Lasting Impact of Stories in Training

Storytelling is one of the most powerful tools an instructor can use to engage, connect, and teach. Stories make abstract concepts concrete, challenge learners to think critically, and create emotional resonance that ensures lessons are remembered and applied. By starting with a story, particularly through the S.T.A.R.T. framework, instructors can hook their audience's attention, setting the tone for a session that is both meaningful and transformative. As trainers master the art of storytelling, they can move beyond routine instruction to create memorable, impactful learning experiences that leave a lasting impression on their learners.

INSTRUCTOR Z'S PRO TIP: ELEVATING YOUR PRESENTATIONS WITH IVS

Figure 4: Instructor Z speaking at the 2024 ILEETA Conference on Color Management in PowerPoint Design

In my career, I've seen far too many presentations fall flat, blending into the sea of cookie-cutter slide designs that fail to engage or inspire. This is why I've developed a design concept called **Immersive Visual Story (IVS)**. It's not just a technique for creating slides; it's an approach that ensures every presentation you craft stands out from the rest and leaves a lasting impression on your audience.

SO WHAT IS IVS?

At its core, Immersive Visual Story is about combining the timeless principles of storytelling with the magic of visual communication. It's more than just slapping some text and images onto a slide—it's about crafting a *narrative* that draws people in, engages their emotions, and helps them truly connect with the content. Whether you're transferring knowledge, introducing new ideas, or presenting data, IVS infuses life into the presentation and ensures that it resonates.

The Elements of IVS

1. **Purposeful Storytelling**: Every slide should feel like part of a larger journey. Just like a good story, there's a beginning, middle, and end. When crafting your slides, think about the arc of your presentation: where are you starting, what's the climax, and how will you leave your audience changed by the end?

2. **Visual Impact**: Visuals are not just decorations—they are *integral* to the story. Use high-quality images, diagrams, and videos that complement your narrative. The right visuals do more than enhance; they *guide* the audience, helping them to visualize abstract ideas or complex data.

3. **Engagement Through Design**: Your design choices should evoke emotion and keep the audience's attention. Simple tweaks in color, layout, and typography can drastically change how the message is perceived. In IVS, these choices are intentional, ensuring that every element on the slide adds value to the story you're telling.

4. **Dynamic Flow**: Transitions between slides and ideas should be seamless, like chapters in a book. Each slide should build on

the last, with smooth transitions that maintain momentum and keep your audience engaged from start to finish.

MAKING IVS WORK FOR YOU

Although my primary platform of expertise is PowerPoint, the IVS concept is flexible enough to apply to any tool or platform you use. Whether it's Canva, Google Slides, Prezi, or any other presentation software, the principles of IVS can elevate your designs, helping you break away from the norm and create something extraordinary.

Don't just aim to present information—aim to tell a story, immerse your audience in that story, and watch your presentations go from ordinary to exceptional. IVS isn't just a tool: it's a mindset, and once you embrace it, your presentations will never be the same.

This insight represents one of the most effective ways I've found to craft visually engaging, memorable presentations that stand apart from the average PowerPoint. Apply it, experiment with it, and watch how your audience's connection with your content deepens.

INSTRUCTOR Z's FINAL WORD:

Whether you're teaching, sharing data, or delivering a keynote, remember that every slide tells a story—and IVS helps you make that story unforgettable.

CHAPTER 4
TESTIMONIAL—BUILDING TRUST

"Testimonials build trust, trust builds relationships, and relationships build success."
—Zig Ziglar

INTRODUCTION

In *The Ultimate Police Trainer's Playbook: Mastering Impactful Openers and Lasting Closers in Training*, one of the most powerful tools for establishing trust with your audience is the strategic use of testimonials. Whether presented as quotes, personal stories, or statistical data, testimonials bring the content to life, showing how concepts have worked in real-world situations. They are more than persuasive elements—they are essential in validating your content and establishing trust, bridging the gap between theory and practice.

When learners hear how others have applied what they are learning—whether through success or failure—they are more likely to trust both the material and the trainer delivering it. Success stories and cautionary tales alike provide invaluable lessons, making testimonials crucial to a comprehensive training experience.

THE POWER OF SOCIAL PROOF

Social proof is a psychological concept that explains why people tend to trust the experiences of others when making decisions. In training, testimonials function as social proof, offering learners evidence that the techniques or strategies being taught have been effectively applied in real-world scenarios. As Robert Cialdini explains in *Influence: The Psychology of Persuasion*, one of the strongest motivators for decision-making is the principle of social proof. People look to others for validation, especially when uncertain about a course of action.

Consider the case of Sergeant Kevin Briggs, a former California Highway Patrol officer whose story illustrates the profound impact of crisis intervention techniques. Through his calm, empathetic communication on the Golden Gate Bridge, he has been credited with preventing over two hundred suicide attempts. His success shows the life-saving potential of these methods, validating the importance of mastering such skills in real-world, high-pressure environments.

BUILDING CREDIBILITY AND TRUST

When used effectively, testimonials build credibility by showing learners that the concepts being taught are not just theoretical but have been applied successfully by others in real-life situations. This is especially important in high-stakes fields like law enforcement, mental health, or crisis intervention. By sharing both successes and failures, trainers can make the lessons relatable and grounded in reality.

Incorporating testimonials from respected individuals, like Sergeant Briggs, further enhances credibility. When learners hear that someone with his experience has applied these techniques to save lives, it deepens their trust in the trainer and the training process.

LESSONS FROM SUCCESS AND FAILURE

Both success and failure provide meaningful learning opportunities. Success stories inspire learners by demonstrating the positive outcomes of applying best practices. On the other hand, stories of failure serve as cautionary tales, offering lessons about the consequences of neglecting key principles or failing to act under pressure.

For instance, a testimonial from an officer who failed to follow de-escalation techniques during a crisis, resulting in an avoidable escalation, serves as a stark reminder of the importance of using the methods learned. Conversely, hearing how another officer successfully applied the same techniques to prevent a volatile situation from spiraling out of control highlights their value.

CRAFTING COMPELLING TESTIMONIALS

To maximize the impact of a testimonial, it must be carefully crafted to align with the core learning objectives of the training session. A powerful testimonial is not just a story but a narrative that enhances the credibility of the lesson. Here is how to create compelling testimonials:

1. **Specificity Matters**: General statements lack impact. Testimonials should provide specific outcomes and details that reinforce the effectiveness of the training.

Example: "After applying the de-escalation techniques from this course, our department saw a 30 percent reduction in the use of force incidents within six months."

2. **Make It Relatable**: The testimonial should reflect challenges or scenarios that the audience can see themselves facing. This relatability helps learners connect emotionally with the story.

Example: "I was in the same position many of you are in today: burnt out and unsure if these techniques would make a difference. But after using the communication strategies taught here, I've witnessed firsthand how they de-escalate even the most high-pressure situations."

3. **Highlight Authority Figures**: A testimonial from a respected figure or subject matter expert adds significant credibility. It carries more weight when learners recognize and trust the person delivering the message.

Example: "Sergeant Kevin Briggs, known for his life-saving work on the Golden Gate Bridge, attributes much of his success in crisis intervention to the techniques that align closely with what we are covering today."

4. **Incorporate Emotional Appeal**: Emotional testimonials leave a lasting impression, particularly when they tap into feelings of empathy, triumph, or resilience.

Example: "I was destroyed when my own agency turned its back on me after having been cleared of any wrongdoing. I felt betrayed. However, the resilience-building strategies I learned in this course helped me find the strength to move forward, even when it seemed impossible."

5. **Align with Learning Objectives**: The testimonial should directly support the session's key message or learning objective. A well-crafted testimonial that connects with the goals of the training reinforces the value of the content.

Example: If the goal is to improve leadership skills under pressure, the testimonial should highlight how those skills helped in a real crisis: "When my team faced an unexpected crisis, the leadership principles I learned here enabled me to guide them through it successfully."

CONCLUSION

Testimonials are a powerful way to build trust, establish credibility, and reinforce the relevance of the material being taught. They serve as social proof, demonstrating that the concepts are not just theoretical but have been applied successfully—or unsuccessfully—by others, offering tangible lessons for learners. Whether a story of triumph or caution, a well-placed testimonial transforms theory into practice and helps create a meaningful, lasting connection between the trainer and the learner.

In *The Ultimate Police Trainer's Playbook: Mastering Impactful Openers and Lasting Closers in Training*, mastering the art of using testimonials can elevate your training to new levels of engagement and credibility. By incorporating these stories wisely, you build trust with your audience and create a training experience that is not only impactful but also grounded in real-world applications.

CHAPTER 5
ANALOGY—SIMPLIFYING COMPLEX CONCEPTS

"Analogy is to the intellect what color is to the soul: it makes knowledge vivid and memorable."
—Voltaire

Analogies are one of the most powerful tools trainers can use to bridge the gap between complex concepts and learner understanding. In *The Ultimate Police Trainer's Playbook*, the "A" in the S.T.A.R.T. framework represents the use of analogies to craft compelling openers that set the stage for impactful learning. This technique is especially valuable in fields like law enforcement, corrections, and public safety, where concepts can be intricate but clarity and retention are essential.

WHY ANALOGIES MATTER

The human brain naturally connects new information to what it already knows, and analogies tap into this process. By linking unfamiliar or complex ideas to something relatable, analogies simplify learning. Research suggests that analogies help activate prior knowledge and facilitate the processing of new information, improving both comprehension and recall (Gentner, 1983). This is particularly important in high-stakes environments like public safety, where quick decision-making can mean the difference between life and death.

For example, when teaching officers how to respond to stress, comparing their thought processes to the flow of traffic—where stop, proceed with caution, or go are based on external cues—helps simplify a multifaceted idea. These kinds of analogies make the content more digestible and memorable, ensuring learners can recall and apply the information when it matters most.

THE ROLE OF ANALOGIES IN LAW ENFORCEMENT AND PUBLIC SAFETY

In law enforcement and public safety training, officers often need to absorb a range of complex topics, from legal protocols to tactical strategies and psychological frameworks. Analogies serve as a tool to not only simplify these concepts but to make them relatable and easier to internalize. Whether it is in a classroom setting or a field exercise, analogies help anchor understanding so officers can process information quickly and retain it when under stress.

Moreover, analogies work particularly well in environments where high retention and application are crucial. In a field where lives are on the line, having a concrete mental image attached to a complex idea can be the difference between success and failure. According to Mayer (2002), analogies also promote meaningful learning, as they allow learners to relate abstract concepts to familiar experiences.

CRAFTING EFFECTIVE ANALOGIES FOR POLICE TRAINING

To ensure analogies resonate, they must be:

- **Relatable**: The analogy should connect the new concept to something the learner already knows or experiences regularly.
- **Simple**: Avoid making the analogy more complex than the concept itself.
- **Applicable**: Ensure the analogy can be directly applied to real-world scenarios officers might face.

Here are some examples of how analogies can enhance police training:

1. **Traffic Light and Decision Making**:
   "Just as a driver must make split-second decisions at a traffic light—stop, proceed cautiously, or go—officers face similar choices in high-stress situations." This analogy can help simplify the decision-making process under pressure, encouraging officers to act with both urgency and caution.

2. **Camera Focus and Situational Awareness**:
   "Compare situational awareness to adjusting the focus on a camera lens. At times, officers need a wide-angle view to observe everything around them, while at other times, they need to zoom in on the smallest details." This analogy is useful in tactical training, where attention to both the big picture and finer points is critical.

3. **Jigsaw Puzzle and Evidence Gathering**:
   "Like solving a jigsaw puzzle, evidence collection requires patience and precision. Officers may not immediately understand how all the pieces fit together, but with time and persistence, the full picture will emerge." This analogy helps reduce frustration during lengthy investigations and emphasizes the value of methodical work.

4. **Building a House and Leadership Development**:
   "Leadership is like building a house—it requires a solid foundation (values and integrity), reliable tools (skills and knowledge), and consistent upkeep (ongoing learning and development). Just as a well-built house stands the test of time, strong leadership endures through challenges." This analogy highlights leadership as a process built on strong values, essential skills, and continuous learning, emphasizing the need for a solid foundation and ongoing development to endure challenges.

5. **Waves in an Ocean and Stress Management**:
   "Stress in law enforcement is like waves in the ocean—sometimes small and manageable, other times overwhelming. Officers, like surfers, must learn to ride the waves without being swept away." This analogy helps officers normalize the stress they experience on the job and develop coping mechanisms.

IMPLEMENTING ANALOGIES IN OPENERS

Incorporating analogies as part of your training opener primes learners to engage with the material. Analogies not only simplify complex ideas but also make the information more memorable. This is crucial in high-pressure environments like law enforcement, where officers need to internalize knowledge quickly and apply it under stress.

CONCLUSION

Analogies are a critical tool in any trainer's playbook. They take complex, often abstract, ideas and make them understandable and actionable. In law enforcement, corrections, and public safety, where knowledge can directly affect officer safety and public welfare, analogies help simplify learning and make concepts stick.

As we have seen in this chapter, analogies used in the S.T.A.R.T. framework can transform the way information is delivered and understood. By incorporating them into your openers, you are not just explaining—you are equipping your learners with the tools to retain and apply vital knowledge in the field.

CHAPTER 6
RHETORICAL QUESTION— SPARKING REFLECTION

"Asking the right questions takes as much skill as giving the right answers."
—Robert Half

Rhetorical questions are a powerful tool in training because they invite learners to pause, reflect, and engage with the material on a deeper level. Unlike direct questions that demand an answer, rhetorical questions are designed to provoke thought, encouraging learners to critically assess their own knowledge, beliefs, and assumptions. By engaging their minds in this way, you create a learning environment that is interactive and dynamic without the need for immediate verbal responses.

WHY USE RHETORICAL QUESTIONS?

Rhetorical questions serve several key functions in the learning process:

1. **Stimulating Curiosity**: They pique learners' interest and draw them into the material by prompting internal dialogue. When a rhetorical question is asked, learners instinctively begin to search

for answers within their own experiences or knowledge, making the session feel more personally relevant.

2. **Encouraging Critical Thinking**: These questions challenge the learner to move beyond surface-level understanding. Instead of merely absorbing information, they begin to analyze it, consider different perspectives, and evaluate its application in real-world scenarios.

3. **Creating Emotional Connection**: Rhetorical questions can tap into emotions, particularly when they touch on ethical, moral, or deeply personal subjects. This emotional engagement helps anchor the lesson, making it more memorable and impactful.

4. **Enhancing Retention**: By involving learners in mental exercise, rhetorical questions help reinforce key concepts. They lead to deeper cognitive processing, which can improve both comprehension and retention.

HOW TO INCORPORATE RHETORICAL QUESTIONS INTO TRAINING

In *The Ultimate Police Trainer's Playbook: Mastering Impactful Openers and Lasting Closers in Training*, rhetorical questions are a key element of the S.T.A.R.T. framework. Using them in openers sets the stage for a more engaged learning experience. The key to using them effectively lies in their relevance to the subject and ability to spark thoughtful reflection. Here are some strategies for incorporating rhetorical questions:

1. **Connect with Core Values**: Rhetorical questions that tap into the learner's core values or professional standards are particularly effective in training environments. These questions challenge

participants to consider the ethical dimensions of their roles and responsibilities.

2. **Highlight Real-World Relevance**: Questions that directly relate to practical, real-world situations compel learners to think about how the material will impact their day-to-day work.

3. **Challenge Assumptions**: By using rhetorical questions to question commonly held assumptions, you encourage learners to break free from rote thinking and consider alternative approaches or perspectives.

Examples of Rhetorical Questions in Training

Here are some sample rhetorical questions that could be effectively used in various training environments:

- **For Leadership Training**: *"What would happen if we all waited for someone else to step up and lead during a crisis?"*
- **For Ethics Training**: *"If no one is watching, do the rules still matter?"*
- **For Officer Safety Training**: *"How much can you afford to lose when hesitation takes over in a critical moment?"*
- **For Burnout Awareness Training**: *"What do you sacrifice when you never allow yourself to rest?"*
- **For Communication Skills Training**: *"Is it enough to speak the truth, or do we need to consider how our words are received?"*

Each of these questions is designed to create a moment of pause, pushing learners to reflect on their role, their choices, and the potential consequences of their actions.

THE COGNITIVE IMPACT OF RHETORICAL QUESTIONS

Research supports the use of rhetorical questions as an effective instructional tool. According to educational psychologist Dr. A.L. Brown, rhetorical questions trigger metacognition, the process of thinking about one's thinking. This metacognitive reflection helps learners not only absorb information but also understand their cognitive process and decision-making (Brown, 1987).

Moreover, a study conducted by R.C. Mayer et al. (1995) found that rhetorical questions can significantly enhance comprehension and retention of material when used strategically throughout a presentation. These questions, when interspersed throughout a lesson, guide learners through complex material by prompting them to mentally rehearse key points (Mayer et al., 1995).

CONCLUSION

Rhetorical questions are more than just a conversational tool: they are a strategic component of impactful training. When used in the right context, they can transform passive listening into active engagement, encouraging learners to critically analyze their roles, decisions, and actions. The "R" in the S.T.A.R.T. framework for impactful openers truly comes alive when rhetorical questions are used to spark reflection, setting the stage for a deeper, more meaningful learning experience.

CHAPTER 7
TAKEAWAY—SETTING LEARNING EXPECTATIONS

"Clarity precedes success."
—Robin Sharma

Setting clear learning expectations at the beginning of a training session is essential to guide learners and keep them invested throughout. In law enforcement and corrections, trainers often face a unique challenge: many officers are not attending voluntarily but are instead "voluntold" by superiors to participate. This widespread practice requires trainers to break through initial resistance and engage participants from the start. One of the most effective ways to do this is by presenting well-constructed, clear key takeaways at the outset.

THE IMPORTANCE OF CLEAR TAKEAWAYS

Key takeaways provide a roadmap for what learners can expect to gain from the session. By laying out these expectations, trainers can help participants see the value of the material and how it connects to their professional duties. According to Malcolm Knowles' *Adult Learning Theory*, adults are most motivated to learn when the content is relevant to their immediate roles and goals (Knowles, 1980). By framing takeaways around practical, real-world applications, you answer the question that is on most learners' minds: *"What's in it for me?"*

When learners know what they will walk away with, they feel more engaged and focused, even if they did not initially choose to attend. Research shows that presenting clear objectives at the beginning of a session increases engagement, encourages deeper cognitive processing, and enhances long-term retention (Ambrose et al., 2010). This is particularly important in law enforcement training, where participants may be entering the session with preconceived notions or resistance, especially around topics like **ethics**, **stress management**, or **cultural sensitivity**.

USING THE "T" IN THE S.T.A.R.T. FRAMEWORK

The last "T" in the *S.T.A.R.T. framework*—Takeaway—plays a critical role in crafting impactful and effective openers. Sharing key takeaways at the beginning of a session not only provides direction but also energizes learners for the journey ahead. For example, consider a training session on **de-escalation techniques**. Instead of diving directly into theory, start by saying:

"Today, you'll leave with three actionable de-escalation techniques that you can immediately apply on your next shift to increase safety for both you and the public."

By offering tangible, applicable skills right away, you frame the training as a valuable opportunity rather than an obligation. This approach helps lower resistance, especially for learners who may have been "voluntold" to attend.

According to a study by Noe (2017), resistance to training is often caused by a disconnect between the perceived relevance of the material and the learner's role. When instructors make the learning objectives clear and tie them to practical applications, learners are more likely to engage and internalize the material. This is why linking takeaways to real-world scenarios is so important—officers need to understand how the training will benefit their daily work.

ADDRESSING PRECONCEPTIONS AND LOWERING RESISTANCE

Many officers may enter a session with preconceived notions about the subject matter. For instance, when faced with a topic like stress management, some officers might think, "I've heard this all before." A well-crafted takeaway can dispel these misconceptions. You might open with something like:

"I know some of you might feel like you've already mastered stress management, but today we'll be covering new, research-backed techniques that will help you stay sharp in high-pressure situations and reduce long-term burnout."

By addressing common reservations early on, you make space for curiosity and interest. Research shows that when learners see the relevance of the training to their own challenges, they are more likely to engage and stay motivated throughout the session (Merriam & Bierema, 2014).

KEEPING IT ACTIONABLE AND CONCISE

Clear takeaways should always be actionable and concise. A general rule of thumb is to focus on three to five key takeaways that align with the main learning objectives of the session. For example, in a full-day training, you could summarize the key outcomes like this:

"By the end of today's session, you will have learned three key de-escalation techniques, practical strategies for reducing job-related stress, and new communication tools to improve community interactions."

This type of summary primes learners for what is to come, making them feel more in control of their learning experience and more likely to retain the information. Studies show that concise, focused takeaways improve both engagement and comprehension (Brinkerhoff, 2005).

CREATING RELEVANCE AND DRIVING ENGAGEMENT

Clear, well-framed takeaways not only set expectations but also create relevance. When participants see that the training content directly applies to their roles, they become more invested. In a session on cultural sensitivity, for example, you could introduce the takeaway like this:

"Today, you'll learn simple adjustments in communication that can prevent misunderstandings with the community and reduce escalation in high-stress situations."

By showing how the training ties directly to their work, you turn a potentially resistant learner into an engaged participant. This is crucial in law enforcement, where the stakes of applying new skills are high.

CONCLUSION: THE TAKEAWAY AS A TOOL FOR ENGAGEMENT

In *The Ultimate Police Trainer's Playbook*, we emphasize that a well-constructed takeaway is not just a summary but a tool for engagement.

When shared at the beginning of a session, key takeaways create clarity, lower barriers to participation, and make learning feel relevant and purposeful. In law enforcement training, where resistance can often be high, this technique is invaluable. By tying the takeaways to real-world applications, addressing preconceived notions, and making the content immediately actionable, trainers can transform "voluntold" participants into active, engaged learners.

INSTRUCTOR Z'S PRO TIP: S.T.A.R.T. YOUR OPENER WITH FLEXIBILITY

Now that you have learned about the S.T.A.R.T. framework, it is important to understand that this approach is not rigid. Think of it as a "menu" of options, where you are free to choose one or more elements to craft your opener. You might find that a well-structured story stands on its own, or perhaps an engaging testimonial, a spot-on analogy, or even a thought-provoking rhetorical question will do the trick. In some cases, starting with a testimonial or analogy could naturally flow into a story and then connect with a key takeaway—all within the same opener. And that is perfectly fine!

Figure 5: Select your opener from S.T.A.R.T.

In fact, the one element that often serves as a common thread across all variations is the takeaway. The takeaway helps make sense of your opener, whether it is a story, testimonial, analogy, or rhetorical question. When you conclude your opener with a powerful takeaway, you give meaning to everything that came before it.

So feel free to be creative! Do not limit yourself to just one element. And remember, you are not simply thinking "outside the box"—you are acknowledging there is no box. Raise the bar, set your own standard, and use the S.T.A.R.T. framework to craft an impactful opener every time.

INSTRUCTOR Z's PRO TIP: MAINTAINING MOMENTUM AFTER THE OPENER

Once you have deployed your opener, whether it was a story, testimonial, analogy, rhetorical question, or takeaway, your job is not finished. You have only ensured a smooth and pleasant takeoff, but this is just the beginning of the flight. The opener sets the tone and frames the problem, creating a compelling "why" for your audience. It primes your students to understand why they need to listen before you have even explained what they will receive.

Now, it is crucial to build on the momentum you have created. Follow the opener with a confident introduction that answers the question everyone wants to know: "Who are you, and why are you the best person to be in front of them?" This brief introduction builds credibility and connection.

Next, depending on the training session, pass the microphone to the students. Do not treat student introductions as a routine task. Instead, use this moment as an opportunity to learn more about your audience—their motivations, past experiences, current mindset, and expectations for the session. This is a vital step toward understanding your students and tailoring your approach to meet their needs.

After introductions, share the agenda for the day, the session, or the week. This step answers the fundamental human need to know what to expect and establishes clear expectations for how the day will unfold. With the stage set, both you and your audience are now aligned, working as a well-oiled unit toward the same goal.

Once you have covered these foundational elements, it is time to dive into the content of your training session. This is where you move forward with confidence, transitioning to the core of your presentation. Regardless of the setting—whether it is a classroom, firing range, mat room, shoot house, computer room, or conference hall—this is where the magic happens. It is in this part of the journey that the content transforms into something impactful, delivering on the promise you set with your opener. Keep your students engaged and connected, making sure they feel like active participants in the learning experience. As always, ensure you guide them through the power of here and now in your training session.

CHAPTER 8
TEACHING BY DESIGN VS. TEACHING BY DEFAULT

> *"Design is not just what it looks like and feels like. Design is how it works."*
> —Steve Jobs

In the previous chapters of *The Ultimate Police Trainer's Playbook: Mastering Impactful Openers and Lasting Closers in Training*, we explored in depth the structure and key components of the S.T.A.R.T. framework, designed to help instructors create powerful, engaging training openers. Now, it is time to take a closer look at some critical concepts that will deepen your understanding of the framework as I originally intended it to be when I developed it. These concepts will enable instructors to fully embrace the framework and apply it more effectively in their sessions.

Figure 6: Be intentional when selecting the path of teaching you will take: ensure it is student-centered

TEACHING BY DESIGN: THE POWER OF INTENTIONALITY

Teaching by design means approaching every aspect of instruction with intentionality. It is not limited to the act of delivering content but extends to all the preparation that takes place beforehand. This includes everything from setting up the venue and organizing materials to preparing multimedia elements—whether it is PowerPoint, Prezi, Google Slides, or Canva. Each of these elements should serve the learning objectives and contribute to an optimal learning environment.

Intentional design involves deliberate actions. Every decision—from how you arrange the room to how you format your slides—should be made with the goal of enhancing the learning experience. Research in educational psychology tells us that well-designed learning environments significantly improve knowledge retention and application (Mayer, 2020).

Instructors who teach by design create an experience that actively supports learners' growth and success.

On the other hand, teaching by default means going through the motions. It is the easy route—using the same templates, same methods, and same uninspired delivery that everyone else uses. This leads to mediocrity, not just in the presentation, but in the learning outcomes. Studies confirm that learners disengage when they perceive material as generic or irrelevant, resulting in reduced comprehension and lower motivation to apply the knowledge (Clark & Mayer, 2016). Instructors who teach by default miss the opportunity to engage learners meaningfully.

THE DANGER OF "ONSTAGE COMPLACENCY"

Far too often, there are instructors who operate under the false belief that the title of 'instructor' alone makes them effective. They assume that by virtue of holding this title, they have earned credibility without needing to constantly improve or innovate. This mindset leads to what I call "onstage complacency." These instructors play the part but do not back it up with continuous development or the drive to evolve. They simply check the boxes, sticking to the "way we do things" and settling for the bare minimum.

Complacency in the police world is not limited to field operations—it exists among instructors as well. Instructors who refuse to adapt, grow, and challenge the status quo end up stuck in mediocrity, becoming "a dime a dozen" type of educators. They rely on outdated methods and put minimal effort into their preparation, which affects their learners' ability to grow and improve. True instructors, however, push beyond the minimum standards and strive to set new benchmarks of excellence. They are deliberate, constantly seeking ways to elevate their instruction and the learning experience.

THE "YOU-NIQUE" INSTRUCTOR

One of the keys to teaching by design is being what I call "YOU-nique." Each instructor has their own personality, charisma, and talents—these traits should be harnessed and integrated into their teaching. Far too many instructors fall into the trap of pretending they are just like every other instructor, playing it safe and blending in. But in doing so, they miss the chance to be memorable and impactful.

Being "YOU-nique" means leveraging your unique qualities to create an engaging, authentic learning experience. Learners remember instructors who bring something special to the table—whether it is humor, storytelling, or practical insights. When you embrace your individuality, you go beyond mere instruction—you create a transformative experience for your learners.

PREPARATION: SETTING THE STAGE FOR SUCCESS

Intentional teaching starts long before you step in front of your audience. Preparation is the foundation of a successful learning session. This includes:

1. **Venue Setup**: The physical environment plays a crucial role in learning. Ensuring that the room is well-lit, organized, and conducive to interaction sets the stage for a productive session (Marzano, 2017).

2. **Material Design**: Whether you are handing out worksheets or designing slides, every element must serve a purpose. Avoid clutter and unnecessary filler content that distracts from the core message (Rosenshine, 2012).

3. **Multimedia**: Use technology thoughtfully to enhance learning, not overwhelm it. Multimedia learning principles show that combining meaningful visuals with text improves comprehension, but excess information or irrelevant animations can hinder understanding (Mayer, 2014).

4. **Instructor Mindset**: Your presence and energy are key. When you show up with enthusiasm, confidence, and a clear vision, your learners are more likely to be engaged and inspired (Patrick, Turner, & Meyer, 2003).

BREAKING FREE FROM DEFAULT TEACHING

The choice between teaching by design and teaching by default is ultimately a decision about how committed you are to your role as an instructor. Those who teach by default settle for what is easy, following the path of least resistance. They avoid change, relying on the same old practices and thinking they can coast on their title alone. However, this approach limits both their own growth and the learning potential of their students.

In contrast, teaching by design requires conscious effort, attention to detail, and a deep commitment to excellence. It means continually refining your craft, evolving your methods, and embracing your "YOU-nique" traits to create memorable and impactful learning experiences. This is not just about checking a box—it is about making a real difference in the lives of those you train.

Instructors who teach by design raise the bar not only for themselves but for their learners. They reject mediocrity and challenge the status quo, striving to deliver sessions that leave a lasting impact. If you aspire to be an instructor who inspires, motivates, and transforms, you must make the deliberate choice to teach by design.

CHAPTER 9
SLIDE DESIGN VS. SLIDE DECORATION—CRAFTING VISUAL SYMPHONIES

"The ability to simplify means to eliminate the unnecessary so that the necessary may speak."
—Hans Hofmann

One of the greatest rewards I have experienced as an instructor is when students or conference attendees approach me after a presentation and ask, "What system did you use?" or "Was your presentation a video?" They are not referring to the content alone—they are captivated by the seamless harmony between the slides and my delivery. Some have said it felt like watching a symphony unfold. This level of engagement does not come from decoration but from the power of intentional *slide design*, where each visual element is carefully crafted to support, rather than replace, the spoken message.

In this chapter, we will explore how intentional slide design is not only key to delivering engaging presentations but also critical to creating impactful openers and memorable closers. When done right, your slides will become an extension of your narrative, allowing your audience to fully immerse themselves in the experience; if your students cannot tell where one slide ends and another begins, then you are doing it right.

SLIDE DECORATION: THE EASY BUT INEFFECTIVE PATH

When most people create slides, they focus on making them look "good" by adding decorative elements like extravagant fonts, super bright colors, and over-the-top animations. This is what I call *slide decoration*. It is a superficial approach, where aesthetics are prioritized over functionality. In this process, instructors often clutter their slides with too much text, irrelevant images, and complex transitions that distract rather than support the message.

These types of slides lead to what I call *Slide Karaoke*—where the presenter ends up reading the content verbatim off the screen, turning their back on the audience and reducing the entire session to a recitation. This approach not only disengages the audience but also diminishes the effectiveness of the learning experience. As Nancy Duarte (2012) explains in her book *Slideology*, "The more text on a slide, the less your audience will remember what you say."

SLIDE DESIGN: INTENTIONAL AND PURPOSEFUL

Intentional slide design is the opposite of decoration. It is about creating slides that *serve a purpose*—slides that are functional, visually appealing, and perfectly aligned with the spoken message. When your slide design is intentional, each element has a reason to be there. It is not just about adding images or text for the sake of filling space; it is about reinforcing your message in a way that resonates with your audience.

Here is a core premise I always share in my PowerPoint Design Workshops: *Your slides are not the presentation. You are the presentation.*

You always have been, and you always will be. Keep it that way. But ensure your slide design aligns with the quality of your delivery. A slide should complement your words, not repeat them.

GUIDELINES FOR CREATING ENGAGING SLIDE DESIGNS

1. **Keep Text Minimal and Focus on Key Points:** Your audience did not come to read—they came to listen and engage. Limit text to key phrases or words that support your spoken message. Full sentences belong in your notes, not on your slides.

    o **Tip:** Follow the six-by-six rule—no more than six bullet points per slide and no more than six words per bullet.

2. **Use High-Quality Visuals:** Visuals are powerful tools to reinforce learning, but they must be purposeful. Use images, graphs, or diagrams that clarify or emphasize key points. Avoid generic stock images that do not add value.

    o **Tip:** Ensure visuals are high-resolution and relevant to the content. Studies show that well-designed visuals increase retention by 42 percent (Mayer, 2001).

3. **Leverage Simple Layouts:** Consistency in font, color scheme, and layout across your slides will keep your audience focused on the content, not distracted by visual inconsistencies. Clean, simple designs are more effective than cluttered, complex ones.

    o **Tip:** Use one or two fonts throughout your presentation. Stick to a limited color palette of three or four complementary colors.

4. **Integrate Interactive Elements:** Engage your audience by incorporating questions, prompts, or activities directly into your slides. This encourages active participation and keeps learners invested in the experience.

    o **Tip:** Try using slides as a way to pose a thought-provoking question or challenge that aligns with the content you are about to present.

5. **Ensure Seamless Transitions:** Slide transitions should feel natural, not distracting. Avoid flashy animations and focus on smooth, purposeful transitions that match the pace of your presentation.

    o **Tip:** Use animations only when necessary to reveal key points one at a time. As Reynolds (2008) notes in *Presentation Zen*, less is often more.

6. **Design for Engagement:** Every slide should support engagement, either by reinforcing the message, prompting discussion, or enhancing understanding. The design should be subtle, allowing the instructor's words to take center stage.

    o **Tip:** Do not be afraid to use blank space. A simple, focused slide with a single image or word can have a much greater impact than a crowded slide full of unnecessary elements.

THE ROLE OF DESIGN IN OPENERS AND CLOSERS

Now, let us connect these design principles back to creating impactful openers and lasting closers. The design of your slides plays a critical role in setting the tone at the beginning and wrapping up your message with a strong, memorable finish. An effective opener captures your audience's attention immediately, and your slides should reflect that sense of urgency and importance.

For example, in an opener, a minimalist slide with a single powerful image or a question can ignite curiosity. As John Medina (2014) outlines in *Brain Rules*, "We don't pay attention to boring things." If your opener is not captivating, the rest of your presentation will struggle to engage the audience. The design must complement the story, testimonial, or analogy you are using in the S.T.A.R.T. framework—helping to solidify that critical first impression.

Likewise, in your closing, your slides should reflect the crescendo of your message, leading to a strong, clear call to action. A thoughtfully designed closing slide, with a poignant image or impactful statement, can leave a lasting impression. *Recency* is a powerful effect in learning—the last thing you present often sticks the longest.

CLOSING THOUGHTS: CRAFTING YOUR VISUAL SYMPHONY

As I tell my students in every PowerPoint Design Workshop, "It is not just about putting together a series of slides—it is about transforming a mundane presentation into a *visual symphony*." When your slide design is intentional, purposeful, and seamlessly aligned with your delivery, the audience experiences something much greater than mere information transfer. They are brought on a journey where the slides are part of the orchestra, and you, the instructor, are the conductor.

And that, my fellow trainers, is how you create a learning experience that resonates long after the class is over.

INSTRUCTOR Z'S PRO TIP: UNLOCKING THE POWER OF PURPOSEFUL SLIDE DESIGN

Figure 7: Instructor Z presenting at one of his many PowerPoint Design Workshops

This Pro Tip dives into the realm of PowerPoint slide design, an area where I have positioned myself as an expert, not just as a police trainer but also as a sought-after PowerPoint designer. Many instructors and organizations have outsourced their design work to me, and through these collaborations, I have come to realize that innovation is not the issue for most clients. They often have a clear, creative vision of what they want their slides to look like. These clients are not only innovative but also creatively driven within their own boundaries. However, what they lack is the technical know-how to transform those ideas into polished, professional designs.

For those who do not outsource their work, this challenge becomes even more apparent. They start with a strong concept but lack the design skills to bring it to life. As a result, they rely heavily on default PowerPoint tools—options created for ease of use, which lead to presentations that are more decorated than truly designed. These basic, "user-friendly" features can limit creativity, resulting in ordinary, subpar presentations that fail to stand out.

This is where the critical difference lies: working PowerPoint "by default" versus working PowerPoint "by design." So let us explore how to break free from the limitations of default settings and elevate your presentations with intentional, purposeful design.

We have already discussed the difference between slide design and slide decoration. Now, let us put that into context: No matter how talented or creative an instructor is, if they operate "by default," their final product will end up looking painfully like everyone else's. This is largely because PowerPoint, in its effort to be intuitive and user-friendly, nudges users toward familiar, easy-to-use menu options—think about it: what is the first prompt you see when you open a new slide? "Click to add title" and "Click to add subtitle." And what do we do? We follow these prompts religiously, filling the slide with text, bullet points, and maybe some irrelevant clip art, thinking we are being efficient when, really, we are just repeating the same formula as everyone else. The result? Predictable, uninspired slides.

But here is where it gets worse: this kind of "Death by PowerPoint" is not even the biggest problem anymore. We live in a world where students have developed a "collective immunity" to boring slides. The moment they encounter yet another text-heavy slide, they check out—mentally teleporting to a far-off place. And with smartphones in hand, it is all too easy for them to drift away, finding that instant gratification through the dopamine hits that come with a quick glance at their phones.

Now, do not get me wrong—dopamine is not the enemy here. In fact, engaging presentations can trigger the very same pleasure and reward centers in the brain. Science shows that well-designed multimedia presentations can activate neurotransmitters like dopamine, serotonin, and even norepinephrine, enhancing attention and reinforcing memory retention (Mayer, 2020). When a presentation is visually appealing and interactive, it stimulates these pathways, making the learning experience multidimensional and more effective (Clark & Mayer, 2016).

So how do we make sure our presentations are dopamine-inducing in a positive way instead of pushing students to their phones? It all comes down to design. Here are my Ten Commandments of PowerPoint Design, principles I use in every slide deck I create:

INSTRUCTOR Z's TEN COMMANDMENTS OF POWERPOINT DESIGN

1. Know Your Audience

Tailor your slides to your audience's knowledge level, interests, and needs. Relevance is everything.

2. One Message Per Slide

Avoid essay-like text on slides. One clear message per slide will make your content digestible.

3. Use Readable Fonts (No Smaller Than Thirty-Two-Point Size)

Choose sans-serif fonts that are clear and easy to read. Avoid fancy or overly stylized fonts that may be hard to decipher at a distance. Also never use a font size smaller than thirty-two points. This ensures that your audience can comfortably read the text without unnecessary eye strain, no matter where they are sitting in the classroom.

4. Use Animations Sparingly

A little animation can bring life to your presentation, but too much can be a distraction. Pick one animation style and stick with it.

5. Moderate Transitions Over Animations

Transitions between slides should be smooth and consistent. Avoid distracting your audience with wild effects.

6. Follow the Six-by-Six Rule

Whenever rule # 2 is not possible and you still have to use bullet points, limit slides to six bullet points, each no more than six words. Keep it concise.

7. Do Not Scale Down Pictures

Go full screen with images. The "picture superiority effect" means people are far more likely to remember information when it is accompanied by a powerful visual (Paivio, 1991).

8. Master the Laws of Color (Contrast, Consistency, and Distribution)

Color is not just for looks—it influences emotions and focus. Use color contrast to make text pop, consistency for visual harmony, and wise color distribution to avoid overwhelm. Tapping into the psychology of color can enhance engagement and retention.

9. Use Full-Slide Videos

Ensure videos in your PowerPoint take up the full screen and play automatically to avoid disrupting the flow. Avoid using URLs, as relying on an internet connection can cause delays and break engagement. Embedding videos directly creates a seamless, uninterrupted experience for your audience.

10. Slides Are Free—Use Them

Do not overcrowd your slides. Create as many as you need to keep content manageable and visually appealing.

Now that you have these ten principles, remember that practice and mastery of structure are crucial for a smooth, seamless presentation. Your goal should be to give your students the impression they are watching a well-produced film rather than flipping through boring stills on an outdated slide projector.

Be intentional with your design and deliberate in your delivery because every slide you create is an opportunity to captivate and inspire. If you're ready to take your presentations from ordinary to extraordinary, I'm here to help. I have crafted courses designed to elevate both the art and science of PowerPoint Design, transforming the way you engage and teach. Let us collaborate to turn your presentations into powerful tools that not only hold attention but leave a lasting impact.

Your PowerPoint slides are not the presentation—you are. You have always been the star, and you always will be. Your slides are simply tools to elevate your delivery. But beware—poorly designed slides can drain the energy from your performance. Put the same passion and effort into your slide design as you do into your delivery because both need to shine for a truly impactful presentation.

CHAPTER 10

THE POWER OF PERSUASION— LEVERAGING ETHOS, PATHOS, AND LOGOS IN YOUR OPENERS AND CLOSERS

> *"People will forget what you said, people will forget what you did, but people will never forget how you made them feel."*
> —Maya Angelou

In this chapter, we will explore how Aristotle's three modes of persuasion—**ethos**, **pathos**, and **logos**—are deeply embedded in the **S.T.A.R.T.** and **E.N.D.I.T.** frameworks. These rhetorical strategies are essential for crafting impactful openers and memorable closers. For law enforcement, corrections, and public safety audiences, where skepticism is high and scrutiny is constant, understanding these persuasive techniques is crucial to engage and retain the audience's attention.

Ethos is particularly significant for these audiences, as credibility is everything in professions that constantly evaluate the trustworthiness and authority of their instructors. Aristotle emphasized the importance of ethos, noting that the personal character of the speaker can be the most effective means of persuasion (*Rhetoric*, 350 BCE). This holds especially true for competitive, skeptical groups like law enforcement officers, who value authenticity and expertise more than anything else.

ETHOS: BUILDING CREDIBILITY FROM THE START

Ethos, or the appeal to credibility, is foundational in law enforcement training. Aristotle defined ethos as the speaker's character and credibility, arguing that audiences are more likely to be persuaded by someone they perceive as trustworthy and knowledgeable (*Rhetoric*, 350 BCE). Establishing ethos is paramount, as officers will quickly assess whether the trainer has the authority and experience to lead them.

The **S.T.A.R.T.** framework—**Story**, **Testimonial**, **Analogy**, **Rhetorical Question**, and **Takeaway**—is designed to build ethos from the outset. Losing credibility early on means losing engagement, which is why it is critical to demonstrate authority immediately. Here's how ethos plays into each component:

- **Story**: Sharing a personal, real-world experience adds credibility because it shows that you have faced similar situations to those of your audience. As Chip and Dan Heath explain in *Made to Stick*, stories are powerful tools for persuasion because they create a connection based on shared experiences (Heath & Heath, 2007). When your audience knows you have been where they are, they are more likely to trust you.
- **Testimonial**: Testimonials from respected peers or leaders are invaluable for establishing ethos. They provide third-party validation, which according to James Kouzes and Barry Posner in *The Leadership Challenge*, helps solidify credibility, especially in skeptical environments (Kouzes & Posner, 2017). Officers value endorsements from those they respect.

- **Analogy**: Using analogies to simplify complex concepts reinforces your expertise and communication skills. Aristotle noted that using analogies helps clarify difficult ideas, making the speaker seem both knowledgeable and relatable (*Rhetoric*, 350 BCE).
- **Rhetorical question**: Posing a rhetorical question related to the audience's challenges signals that you understand their world, which builds trust and establishes credibility. As Carmine Gallo explains in *The Storyteller's Secret*, rhetorical questions can provoke thought and establish rapport with the audience (Gallo, 2016).
- **Takeaway**: Even in the takeaway, ethos is key. By summarizing actionable, relevant insights early in the session, you demonstrate that your session is valuable and structured, which further enhances your authority.

In the **E.N.D.I.T.** framework, ethos remains critical as you **Nail down key takeaways**, **Drive action**, and **Inspire with a statement**. Your credibility must remain intact throughout the session so that when the closing comes, your audience feels confident in the material and in your authority. This ensures that your closer leaves a lasting impact and motivates action.

PATHOS: TAPPING INTO EMOTION TO ENGAGE YOUR AUDIENCE

Pathos, the appeal to emotion, is a powerful tool for engaging your audience. Aristotle argued that emotions can alter our judgments, making pathos a critical element in persuasive communication (*Rhetoric*, 350 BCE). In law enforcement training, tapping into emotions like pride, duty, and fear can create a deep connection between you and your audience.

In the **S.T.A.R.T.** framework, pathos helps you connect with your audience on an emotional level:

Story: Sharing a story with emotional depth can create a bond between the trainer and the audience. According to Gallo, stories that evoke emotions are among the most effective ways to engage listeners (Gallo, 2016). For example, sharing a moment of personal challenge or triumph in your career can stir emotions and make your message resonate.

- **Testimonial**: When you share a testimonial that highlights the emotional impact of your training, you not only build credibility but also engage the audience's emotions. Heath and Heath also emphasize that emotionally driven stories are more memorable and impactful (Heath & Heath, 2007).
- **Analogy**: Emotional analogies, such as comparing high-stress situations to universal human struggles, can evoke empathy and reflection. This aligns with Aristotle's view that analogies help make abstract ideas more relatable (*Rhetoric*, 350 BCE).
- **Rhetorical Question**: A rhetorical question that touches on a personal challenge—such as "What would you do if your backup didn't arrive on time?"—forces your audience to engage emotionally, prompting them to reflect on their own experiences.
- **Takeaway**: Even the takeaway can connect emotionally by reinforcing the human stakes involved. As Kouzes and Posner explain, effective takeaways should not only summarize key points but also connect with the audience's deeper motivations (Kouzes & Posner, 2017).

In the **E.N.D.I.T.** framework, pathos is crucial when you **Inspire with a statement**. By closing on an emotionally resonant note, such as invoking the pride officers feel in their duty, you can leave a lasting impression.

This emotional appeal helps ensure that your audience remembers your message long after the session ends.

LOGOS: APPEALING TO LOGIC AND REASON

Logos, or the appeal to logic, is central to delivering a clear, actionable message. Aristotle argued that logos, the logical appeal, persuades by using reason and evidence (*Rhetoric*, 350 BCE). Law enforcement officers expect content that is practical, evidence-based, and logical. Your audience needs clear, structured arguments they can apply directly to their work.

In the **S.T.A.R.T.** framework, logos is critical in making sure your audience understands the logic behind your content:

- **Story**: Stories should have a logical point that connects directly to the lesson you are teaching. Heath and Heath argue that stories grounded in logic and real-world applications are the most effective because they provide a framework for understanding complex concepts (Heath & Heath, 2007).
- **Testimonial**: Testimonials that provide measurable results or evidence-based outcomes appeal to logos. Law enforcement audiences value logical, evidence-based testimonials that show the practical application of the lesson.
- **Analogy**: Using analogies to simplify complex concepts helps your audience understand the logical connections between the material and their own experiences. Aristotle noted that analogies are effective tools for helping listeners reason through new ideas (*Rhetoric*, 350 BCE).
- **Rhetorical Question**: A rhetorical question designed to prompt critical thinking engages your audience's logical

reasoning. According to Gallo, thought-provoking questions encourage listeners to reflect on logical solutions (Gallo, 2016).
- **Takeaway**: The takeaway is where logos often shines brightest. Summarizing the key points in a logical, structured way ensures that your audience walks away with clear, actionable knowledge. Kouzes and Posner emphasize that clear, structured takeaways are crucial for ensuring the audience retains the material and understands how to apply it (Kouzes & Posner, 2017).

In the **E.N.D.I.T.** framework, logos is central when you **Nail down key takeaways** and **Drive action**. Providing a logical summary and clear steps for applying the material helps your audience understand how to implement what they have learned. A structured, logical closer ensures that your message is not only understood but also actionable.

EMBRACING THE CHALLENGE: WINNING OVER A TOUGH AUDIENCE

Law enforcement officers are a tough audience, known for their competitiveness, skepticism, and scrutiny. However, instead of seeing this as an obstacle, embrace it as a challenge to refine your craft. By mastering ethos, pathos, and logos in your openers and closers, you can captivate even the most difficult audiences.

The **S.T.A.R.T.** and **E.N.D.I.T.** frameworks are not just acronyms—they are powerful tools for delivering persuasive, compelling training sessions. By balancing ethos (credibility), pathos (emotion), and logos (logic), you can transform the way you engage your audience from the first moment to the last, ensuring your message resonates long after the class is over.

CHAPTER 11
THE SIX LAWS OF LEARNING— YOUR FOUNDATION FOR S.T.A.R.T. AND E.N.D.I.T.

> *"Live as if you were to die tomorrow. Learn as if you were to live forever."*
> —Mahatma Gandhi

In the world of training and instruction, understanding and applying the six laws of learning is essential for creating engaging educational experiences. These laws form the bedrock of successful knowledge transfer and play a pivotal role in shaping how instructors deliver their content. When utilized effectively, they help instructors design sessions that are not only informative but transformative. But how do these laws connect with crafting impactful openers and lasting closers? Let us break down the relevance of the six laws of learning to the S.T.A.R.T. and E.N.D.I.T. frameworks.

THE SIX LAWS OF LEARNING DEFINED

The six laws of learning are well-researched principles derived from the fields of cognitive psychology, neuroscience, and educational theory. They are:

- **Law of Readiness**: Learning occurs when the student is mentally and physically prepared.
- **Law of Exercise**: Repetition strengthens learning, making recall and performance easier.
- **Law of Effect**: Positive reinforcement encourages students to retain information and behaviors.
- **Law of Primacy**: The first thing a learner experiences will be remembered best and longest.
- **Law of Recency**: The most recent learning is often remembered better than earlier content.
- **Law of Intensity**: A more intense or emotionally impactful experience leads to deeper learning.

While these laws may seem abstract, their practical relevance becomes clear when we connect them to the S.T.A.R.T. and E.N.D.I.T. frameworks for openers and closers.

CONNECTING THE LAWS WITH S.T.A.R.T.

The S.T.A.R.T. framework is designed to leverage the cognitive principles of engagement from the very beginning of a session. It encompasses Story, Testimonial, Analogy, Rhetorical Question, and Takeaway as powerful elements of an Impactful opener. Each law of learning finds its place within this framework:

- **Law of Primacy**: The opener, governed by the law of primacy, sets the stage for the entire learning experience. First impressions matter, and starting with a purposeful **Story** or **Analogy** ensures that the learner's attention is captured right from the start, embedding early and critical ideas into long-term memory (Gagne, 1985; Baddeley, 2000).
- **Law of Readiness**: A well-crafted **Testimonial** or **Rhetorical Question** primes the learner's mind, preparing them to absorb the forthcoming information. It taps into emotional and intellectual curiosity, enhancing readiness (Willingham, 2009). Learners who are psychologically prepared are more likely to engage deeply and retain information.
- **Law of Intensity**: Starting with a gripping **Story** or powerful **Testimonial** adds emotional intensity, which stimulates engagement and fosters deeper retention (LeDoux, 2002). It activates both cognitive and affective processing, laying the foundation for rich, memorable learning experiences.

CONNECTING THE LAWS WITH E.N.D.I.T.

The E.N.D.I.T. framework ensures that sessions close on a high note, reinforcing key takeaways and leaving learners energized. It emphasizes Ensuring no questions remain, Nailing down key takeaways, Driving action, Inspiring with a statement, and Tying everything together.

- **Law of Recency**: The importance of closing a session effectively ties directly into the law of recency. By **Nailing down key takeaways** and delivering a final **Inspiring statement**, you are ensuring that the most recent experiences are the ones learners will carry with them (Roediger & Butler, 2011).
- **Law of Effect**: An uplifting and actionable call to **Drive action** aligns with the law of effect, which asserts that learners are more

likely to retain information that is followed by a positive emotional experience. Encouraging learners to act on their new knowledge fosters confidence and motivation (Thorndike, 1932).
- **Law of Exercise**: By repeating and reinforcing the critical points during the **Tie it all together** step, you are employing the law of exercise. Repetition strengthens neural pathways and enhances retention (Ebbinghaus, 1913). The closing should repeat key concepts in a meaningful and memorable way.

SEAMLESSLY APPLYING THE SIX LAWS

At first, navigating these laws may seem overwhelming. You might wonder how you can be fully conscious of each law as you craft your openers and closers. However, like any skill, the more you integrate these laws into your training, the more naturally they will guide your teaching. In time, these principles will become second nature—seamless and smooth. Just as repetition strengthens learning for students, the consistent application of these laws will strengthen your instructional design.

I can speak to this from personal experience. Whether I am presenting at conferences or teaching in a conventional classroom, applying the six laws has significantly improved my delivery. These laws have guided me in creating impactful sessions that resonate with students, helping them remember the content and apply it meaningfully in their professional and personal lives.

THE BIGGER PICTURE: ELEVATING STANDARDS FOR OUR STUDENTS AND THEIR FAMILIES

When we elevate the standard and quality of our training, something powerful happens. Our students become reenergized and return to the field equipped with the skills, knowledge, and abilities that will have a lasting, positive impact. They are not only more capable in their roles but they are also better prepared to ensure they make it back home to their loved ones at the end of every mission or shift. If that's not motivation enough for any trainer, then what is?

CHAPTER 12
NAILING THE CLOSER WITH E.N.D.I.T.— FRAMEWORK OVERVIEW.

"You don't close a book without wrapping up the story, and you don't leave a training session without sealing the lessons."
—Antonio Zarzoza

It is often said that the beginning sets the tone, but the ending leaves a lasting impression. A great closing does not just wrap things up neatly: it solidifies learning, motivates action, and ensures that your session will stick in the minds of your participants long after they have left the room. Research shows that the "recency effect," a principle of cognitive psychology, suggests that people are more likely to remember the last piece of information they encounter, especially when it is delivered with impact (Murdock, 1962).

To make sure your sessions end with that kind of power, I developed the **E.N.D.I.T.** framework, which stands for:

- **Ensure no questions remain.**
- **Nail down key takeaways.**
- **Drive action.**
- **Inspire with an evocative statement.**
- **Tie it all together with a clear closer.**

Each element builds on the others to create a cohesive, purposeful closer that leaves no loose ends and ensures maximum retention and engagement.

1. Ensure No Questions Remain

One of the most frustrating experiences for learners is leaving a session with lingering confusion. Ending your session by ensuring there are no unanswered questions is critical for clarity and comprehension. This step emphasizes learner-centered teaching, where instructors create space for questions, review key concepts, and address areas of concern.

Evidence shows that when learners feel comfortable asking questions and have their queries answered, retention rates and overall satisfaction with the learning experience increase (Hattie & Timperley, 2007). During the closer, invite learners to raise any last-minute questions, but ensure this part is controlled and concise to avoid dragging down the momentum. You might say: "Before we conclude, let's make sure everyone is clear on the main points. Does anyone have any questions about today's content?"

2. Nail Down Key Takeaways

The brain can only retain so much information in a brief period. Studies suggest that learners typically retain about 10 percent of the information presented to them unless key points are reiterated in a structured manner (Ebbinghaus, 1885). This is why it is essential to provide a succinct summary of the main points during your closing.

Here, you focus on driving home the most critical concepts. This is not the time to go over everything again but to "nail down" the top two or three takeaways. You can say: "If there's one thing to remember from today, it's X. And remember that Y will help you apply it to Z."

Summarizing in this manner reinforces learning and provides a mental framework for learners to apply the content later. When they leave the session, they will be able to recall these key points, having heard them more than once.

3. Drive Action

The best trainers inspire learners to take action. After all, the goal of any training is not just to deliver information but to drive meaningful change. Behavioral science tells us that people are more likely to act when prompted by specific, actionable steps (Ariely, 2008).

In this step, provide your learners with a clear call to action. This could be something as simple as suggesting they implement a new strategy in the field or challenging them to think differently about a problem. Use specific language to emphasize the action you want them to take: "I challenge you to apply this method in your next team meeting," or "Your next step is to revisit your approach to X based on what you've learned here today."

The key is to create urgency and a sense of responsibility. When learners leave with a clear task in mind, they are more likely to apply what they have learned rather than letting it fade.

4. Inspire with an Evocative Statement

Inspiration is a powerful tool for learning retention. People remember how they feel about something long after they have forgotten the details. Neuroscientific research into emotional engagement suggests that emotion enhances memory retention because it triggers deeper cognitive processing (Tyng et al., 2017).

In this step, you leave your audience with an inspiring thought. This could be a motivational quote, a relevant story, or a thought-provoking statement that resonates with the material. Consider something like, "Remember, leadership isn't about having all the answers but about asking the right questions. Be the leader who sparks change, not just the one who follows it."

Your goal is to leave them thinking, feeling, and energized. The more personal and relatable your statement, the stronger the emotional connection.

5. Tie It All Together with a Clear Closer

Finally, a clear and definitive closer is critical for giving your learners a sense of completion. Leaving your audience with ambiguity at the end of your session can lead to confusion or dissatisfaction. You need to tie all the elements together in a cohesive manner that leaves no doubt the session is over.

Research from communication experts emphasizes the importance of nonverbal cues in signaling the end of a conversation or presentation (Mehrabian, 1972). Using both verbal and nonverbal techniques to signify closure—such as stating clearly, "That wraps up today's session" or thanking your audience—ensures a smooth and confident finish.

The idea here is to make the audience feel they have reached a meaningful conclusion, not a sudden stop. Ending with a confident farewell provides that final piece of satisfaction for your learners.

WHY A MEMORABLE CLOSER IS ESSENTIAL

A strong closing does more than just summarize what has been learned—it reinforces retention, drives motivation, and provides closure, which is key to adult learning. Research shows that without proper closure, learners are left with an incomplete mental framework of the material, which hampers their ability to recall or apply what they have learned (Zull, 2002). By using E.N.D.I.T., you are capitalizing on cognitive principles like the recency effect while ensuring emotional engagement and actionable takeaways.

When you finish with intention, your learners leave your session with clarity, purpose, and motivation, ensuring that the time spent in training was both impactful and transformative.

CHAPTER 13
ENSURE NO QUESTIONS REMAIN

*"The art and science of asking questions
is the source of all knowledge."*
—Thomas Berger

The first step in the E.N.D.I.T. framework, **Ensure no questions remain**, is essential for crafting a memorable and effective closing to any speech, training event, or presentation. This step addresses the critical task of clearing up any confusion and reinforces understanding before moving to the next phase of the closing. Let us explore why this step is so vital, backed by evidence from educational psychology and instructional design.

WHY ENSURING NO QUESTIONS REMAIN IS CRITICAL

It is easy to assume that your message has been fully understood by the time you reach the end of a session, but this assumption can be misleading. Research shows that knowledge retention and comprehension are often solidified during the final moments of a lesson (Hattie & Timperley, 2007). Ensuring no questions remain creates a feedback loop that gives the presenter a final opportunity to address gaps in understanding. This moment is key because learners often refrain from asking questions mid-presentation, either out of reluctance or because they only realize their confusion near the end (Black & Wiliam, 1998).

Cognitive Load Theory suggests that the brain can only manage so much information at once (Sweller, 2011). As learners process new information, cognitive load increases, which can cause key details to slip through the cracks. By pausing to ensure no questions remain, trainers can alleviate cognitive load and strengthen learner recall. This is especially important during the closing, when learners are reviewing everything they have absorbed. This moment allows them to process, ask questions, and clarify points that might have become muddled throughout the session (Sweller, 2011).

Neglecting this step can result in knowledge gaps that reduce the effectiveness of even the most well-planned presentations. Studies have shown that addressing audience questions directly improves retention and learner satisfaction (Chin & Brown, 2000). Failing to do so may leave participants with doubts that linger well beyond the session, reducing their ability to apply the material effectively.

COMMUNICATING THAT UNDERSTANDING MATTERS

By taking time to ensure no questions remain, you are communicating several key messages to your audience:

1. **Their understanding is your priority**: Ensuring there are no unresolved questions shows that you value their learning experience. Adult learners appreciate this attention to detail, as they tend to be independent and purposeful (Knowles et al., 2015).

2. **You are committed to their success**: Taking time for questions at the end emphasizes that the session is not about merely ticking boxes. It is about empowering the audience with the skills and knowledge they need to succeed. Research by Brookfield (2013) highlights that learners feel more confident when they know the instructor cares about their success.

3. **It encourages reflective thinking**: Asking for questions invites learners to reflect on the content, which is an essential aspect of critical thinking. According to King (1991), encouraging reflective questioning promotes deeper understanding and long-term retention.

STRATEGIES FOR ENSURING NO QUESTIONS REMAIN

There are several effective strategies that can be implemented to ensure that no questions remain at the end of your presentation:

1. **Open the floor with purpose**: Avoid a generic "Any questions?" Instead, prompt reflection by saying something like, "What questions do you have about what we've covered?" This phrasing encourages attendees to engage, as it assumes that questions are natural and expected (Tanner, 2013).

2. **Create safe spaces for inquiry**: Some learners may be hesitant to ask questions in a group setting. Providing an anonymous question submission method, such as a digital tool or note card, can encourage more participation (Fry, Ketteridge, & Marshall, 2008).

3. **Summarize before inviting questions**: A brief summary of the key takeaways before asking for questions can jog the memory and spur new questions. This strategy aligns with **The Law of**

Recency, which states that learners retain information presented last more readily than middle content (Thalheimer, 2006).

4. **Check for understanding with reflective prompts**: Ask reflective questions like, "What part of today's session could you see applying immediately?" or "Which concept do you think needs more discussion before we wrap up?" These strategies guide learners to actively think about their learning gaps and can lead to more specific and thoughtful questions (King, 1991).

CONCLUSION

Ensuring no questions remain is not just a formality: it is an integral step in crafting a memorable and effective closing. It emphasizes that you care about your audience's understanding, reduces cognitive overload, and encourages deeper reflection on the material. This step ensures that when you move to the next stages of the E.N.D.I.T. framework, your learners are equipped with clarity, confidence, and the competence to apply what they have learned.

CHAPTER 14
NAIL DOWN KEY TAKEAWAYS

"It is not what is poured into a student that counts, but what is planted."
—Linda Conway

Summarizing key takeaways is essential for ensuring that learners leave with a clear and solid understanding of the material presented. A successful summary is not just a recap—it is an opportunity to reinforce critical lessons, connect the learning journey, and highlight the relevance of the material. In this chapter, we will explore how to effectively summarize takeaways and demonstrate mastery in crafting a cohesive and impactful learning experience.

THE IMPORTANCE OF HIGHLIGHTING KEY LESSONS

Summarizing takeaways is like delivering the final punchline in a well-crafted story. The goal is to ensure that learners can recall and apply the most important concepts or skills. This not only reinforces memory retention but also solidifies learning by guiding students to the aha moments that occurred throughout the session.

According to research on adult learning principles, adults are most likely to retain information when they can immediately see the relevance and practical application of that knowledge (Knowles, 1984). A summary that emphasizes these aspects ensures that learners will carry the lessons with them into the real world.

HOW TO SUMMARIZE EFFECTIVELY

1. **Revisit the Main Objectives:** Your takeaways should align with the learning objectives you presented at the beginning of the session. Remind learners of what was promised at the start to ensure a seamless connection between expectations and outcomes. This creates a sense of closure and satisfaction for the audience, knowing they have accomplished what they set out to learn.

2. **Prioritize the Key Points:** Select two to three main points to focus on. Overwhelming learners with too much information in the summary can dilute its effectiveness. Instead, emphasize the most actionable and relevant takeaways.

3. **Use a Memorable Framework or Mnemonic:** Providing learners with a mental "hook" to remember the key takeaways is an effective technique. This could be in the form of a simple acronym, a metaphor, or a repeating phrase that sums up the core lessons (Sousa, 2011). For example, "Remember: Respond, Reflect, Reframe" for a communication course.

4. **Make It Relatable:** Connect the key takeaways to the real-world challenges learners may face. This reinforces the WIIFM (What's In It For Me?) principle (Dewey, 1938), ensuring that learners understand the personal or professional benefits of applying these takeaways in their own lives.

CONNECTING THE TAKEAWAYS: FROM OPENER TO CLOSER

One of the hallmarks of a well-crafted class is the seamless connection between the takeaways mentioned at the start and those emphasized during the closing. This demonstrates mastery in teaching and provides learners with a sense of completion. Here is how to achieve this connection:

1. **Promised vs. Delivered Takeaways:** At the start of your class, you introduced the main goals or learning outcomes. During the summary, reflect on these initial promises. Highlight how each key takeaway ties back to those original goals. This helps learners feel that the session has come full circle, fostering a sense of accomplishment.

2. **The Culmination of a Journey:** Think of the class as a journey that began with the opener. As you summarize, emphasize how the learners' understanding evolved and highlight how each concept or skill fits into the broader context. This reinforces the flow of learning, reminding learners how far they have come in a brief time.

3. **Echo Your Opener:** If you started with a story, analogy, or rhetorical question, return to it in your closing. This creates a strong psychological link between the beginning and end, helping learners remember both the journey and the lessons (Miller, 1956).

4. **Demonstrate Mastery:** A well-executed summary shows your command over the subject matter and the learning process. By effectively tying in the opener and closing, you highlight that every part of the class was purposefully designed to guide the learner to this final moment. It highlights that the learning experience was not random or disjointed but crafted with intention and expertise.

CRAFTING AN IMPACTFUL SUMMARY

To ensure your summary is impactful and ties in with the broader learning goals, follow these tips:

1. **Ask Reflective Questions:** Engage the learners by asking reflective questions during the summary. For example, "How do you think you can apply these techniques in your daily routine?" This not only reinforces the takeaways but also encourages critical thinking (Brookfield, 1987).

2. **Summarize, Do not Repeat:** Avoid rehashing the entire session. Instead, synthesize the material, bringing the key lessons into sharp focus. Summarize in a way that encourages learners to see the material holistically and appreciate the interconnectedness of the concepts (Caine & Caine, 1994).

3. **End with a Call to Action:** The summary should leave learners motivated and empowered to take action. Frame your key takeaways as steps they can implement immediately, reinforcing their importance and practicality. For example, "Starting tomorrow, try incorporating these de-escalation techniques when engaging with difficult situations."

MASTERING THE CRAFT: A CULMINATION OF SUCCESS

A well-constructed summary is the culmination of a successful learning experience. It brings together the promise made at the beginning of the session and the insights delivered throughout. By nailing down key takeaways and ensuring a strong connection between opener and closer, you will help your learners retain the material and apply it effectively in their daily lives.

Remember, summarizing key lessons is not just about repeating information. It is about crafting a final moment of clarity, where learners leave feeling enriched, empowered, and ready to apply what they have learned. When you take the time to intentionally highlight the most important takeaways, you will not only demonstrate mastery in your craft but also leave a lasting impact on your audience.

CHAPTER 15
DRIVE ACTION

"Vision without action is merely a dream. Action without vision just passes the time. Vision with action can change the world."
—Joel A. Barker

One of the most critical components of a successful training session is the *call to action* (CTA). It is not enough for learners to simply absorb knowledge during the session; they must be empowered and motivated to *apply* that knowledge in their professional or personal lives. This is where action-driven learning comes into play. By guiding learners to take actionable steps after the session, instructors move beyond knowledge transfer and create real-world impact.

In this chapter, we will explore the psychology of action-driven learning, examine examples of motivating CTAs, and provide a framework for crafting CTAs that align with course content, lesson plans, or learning objectives.

THE CASE FOR ACTION-DRIVEN LEARNING

Action-driven learning emphasizes that retention alone is insufficient for creating behavioral change or fostering skill development. Adult learners, in particular, benefit from immediately applying what they have learned because it bridges the gap between theoretical knowledge and practical application. Studies show that when learners take action immediately after learning, they not only retain more information but also experience a higher degree of competency and confidence in executing new skills (Knowles, Holton, & Swanson, 2015). This process engages the *Law of Recency*, which asserts that the most recent learning experience is the one most likely to be remembered and applied. By prompting learners to take immediate action, you reinforce their ability to recall and use the material when it matters most.

Instructors who incorporate calls to action (CTAs) within their lessons empower learners to transition from passive recipients of information to active agents of change. Crafting a CTA is about more than just telling learners what to do—it is about igniting a sense of purpose and urgency.

EXAMPLES OF MOTIVATING CALLS TO ACTION

Below are examples of effective CTAs that inspire learners to take immediate, purposeful action:

1. *"Within the next twenty-four hours, implement at least one of the strategies discussed today. Share your results with a peer or supervisor."*

    o This CTA creates urgency by placing a clear timeframe, ensuring that the material does not fade into the background post session.

2. *"For the next week, practice active listening techniques during your daily interactions with colleagues. Reflect on how it changes your communication style."*

    o This CTA is behavior-focused, encouraging learners to integrate skills gradually into their routines.

3. *"Before our next session, identify one area in your department where the principles from today's class can be applied. Draft a short plan and be prepared to discuss your experience."*

    o This CTA promotes accountability by asking learners to prepare and reflect, thus increasing engagement.

4. *"Send an email to your team outlining three key takeaways from today's session. Include one action you plan to take to improve a process or skill."*

    o This approach is simple yet effective, as it solidifies the learner's understanding and requires public accountability.

CRAFTING CALLS TO ACTION FROM LEARNING OBJECTIVES

To create impactful CTAs, instructors must align them with the course's learning objectives. This ensures that the call to action is relevant and reinforces key takeaways from the session. Here is how to craft an action-driven CTA:

1. **Review the Learning Objectives**: Start by revisiting the course objectives. Each objective should lead to a skill, behavior, or change in mindset that learners can act upon.

For example, if the objective is "learners will be able to demonstrate effective communication techniques in stressful situations," your CTA could be:

"Identify one stressful interaction from the past week and reflect on how you could have communicated differently using today's techniques. Share your insights with a colleague or supervisor."

2. **Use Action Verbs**: A well-crafted CTA utilizes strong, action-oriented verbs. Terms such as "apply," "implement," "reflect," "share," "practice," and "evaluate" signal that the learner must engage with the material actively, not passively. Bloom's Taxonomy provides a valuable guide for selecting these verbs (Anderson & Krathwohl, 2001).

3. **Set a Time frame**: One way to ensure action is taken is by setting a specific time frame. CTAs with deadlines or timelines create a sense of urgency and prevent procrastination. Without a time frame, learners may put off taking action indefinitely (Covey, 1989).

For instance, from a course on time management, if the learning objective is to improve task prioritization, the CTA might be:

"Within the next two days, apply the Eisenhower Matrix to organize your tasks and identify at least two items you can delegate or eliminate."

4. **Tie the Action to Personal or Professional Relevance**: Adult learners are motivated by relevance. The CTA should connect directly to something that matters to the learner's day-to-day life. This principle is based on the *WIIFM* (What's In It For Me?) framework, which reminds learners of the personal or professional benefits of taking action (Keller, 2010).

5. **Keep It Simple, Yet Meaningful**: The call to action should be simple enough for learners to accomplish but meaningful enough to make an impact. Overly complicated or vague CTAs may overwhelm learners and reduce the likelihood of follow-through.

SUGGESTIONS FOR CRAFTING EFFECTIVE CTAS

When brainstorming or crafting CTAs, instructors can follow these strategies:

- **Reflect on the Course's Pain Points**: What problems does the course solve? A CTA should offer learners a pathway to start solving those problems right away. For example, in a crisis intervention course, the CTA could be:

    o "Create a mock scenario where you apply de-escalation techniques from today's lesson. Share your scenario with a peer and practice it together."

- **Ask Open-Ended Questions**: CTAs that challenge learners to think critically or reflect on their individual experiences often spark more profound engagement. These questions could take the form of:

    o "What's one thing you will do differently after today's session to foster better team collaboration? Write it down and implement it this week."

- **Provide Accountability**: Learners are more likely to take action if they know they will be held accountable. Suggest follow-ups such as:

  - "Before the next session, email me a brief reflection on how you applied today's material in a real-world setting."

CONCLUSION

The ultimate goal of any training session is to create lasting change, and that change happens when learners are encouraged to act. By incorporating strong, well-crafted calls to action, instructors can bridge the gap between theoretical learning and real-world application. When learners are given a clear path to follow, along with the motivation and urgency to take action, training becomes more than just a session—it becomes a transformative experience.

Remember: the end of a training session is the beginning of the learner's journey. With effective calls to action, you give your learners the tools, motivation, and drive to make that journey a truly impactful and lasting one.

CHAPTER 16
INSPIRE WITH AN EVOCATIVE STATEMENT

"To awaken human emotion is the absolute pinnacle of art."
—Antonio Zarzoza

Ending a session with an evocative statement offers trainers the opportunity to transcend the typical call to action, leaving a lasting impression that resonates on a deeper, emotional level. While a call to action focuses on what learners must *do*, an evocative statement taps into who they *are* and why it matters. For a highly scrutinizing audience like police officers, this distinction is crucial. A well-crafted, emotion-driven closing speaks to their sense of duty, purpose, and the core values that drive their daily work. It is the difference between instructing and inspiring—between telling them what to do and igniting a fire that will carry them through even the toughest moments on the job.

AWAKENING EMOTION: THE PINNACLE OF ART

One of the most rewarding aspects of teaching is mastering the art of reaching learners within the affective domain—the domain of emotions, attitudes, and values. As I often tell instructors: "To awaken human

EMOTION is the absolute PINNACLE of ART." When you can evoke emotion in your learners, you are not just transferring information; you are transforming how they see the world and their role in it.

Evoking emotion in a closing statement is the highest expression of this art. It is a chance to tie the entire learning experience together by tapping into the heart of why your audience does what they do. In law enforcement training, where officers must constantly balance risk, duty, and public scrutiny, this emotional connection becomes even more essential. It is what helps officers internalize the content and apply it with conviction.

THE POWER OF AN EVOCATIVE CLOSING

Ending a session with an evocative statement creates what psychologists call an "emotional anchor." Research in adult learning consistently shows that emotional experiences enhance retention and engagement. Studies in cognitive neuroscience suggest that when learning is paired with emotional content, it engages deeper cognitive processes, leading to stronger memory formation (Immordino-Yang & Damasio, 2007). When an instructor closes by evoking strong feelings and emotions—whether it is pride, courage, or a renewed sense of purpose—those emotions become tied to the content of the session, making it far more likely that the learner will carry the message forward.

For police officers, connecting the training to their deeper motivations helps ensure that the lessons do not just remain theoretical—they become part of their daily practice. Evocative statements inspire officers to reflect on their purpose, their values, and the noble calling that brought them into the profession in the first place (Knowles, Holton, & Swanson, 2015).

CRAFTING THE EVOCATIVE STATEMENT

When crafting an evocative closing statement, the goal is to stir a sense of emotion and purpose. For police officers, this emotion is often tied to their oath, their commitment to public safety, and their personal sense of justice and service. Here are several elements to keep in mind:

1. **Appeal to Core Values**: Police officers are driven by values like integrity, courage, and a commitment to justice. Your evocative statement should reaffirm these values, reminding officers of their purpose.

   - *Example: "In a world full of noise and distraction, remember this—integrity is your compass, and courage is your constant companion. As long as you follow both, you'll never lose your way."*

2. **Invoke the Collective Mission**: Police work is often about being part of something larger—a collective mission to serve and protect. Evoking that sense of unity can leave officers feeling empowered.

   - *Example: "When the weight of the world feels heavy on your shoulders, remember—you're never standing alone. You are part of a brotherhood, a sisterhood, a family bound by the same unshakable mission: to protect, to serve, and to stand for what's right."*

3. **Link to Personal Growth**: Encourage officers to reflect on their personal growth and evolution. This can deepen their commitment to continuous improvement.

   - *Example: "Every obstacle is an opportunity to grow, to learn, and to become the officer you were meant to be. The road isn't easy, but each step brings you closer to mastering not just your craft, but yourself."*

4. **Inspire Through Emotion**: Close by stirring an emotion that reinforces the importance of their role, connecting it to a sense of pride, responsibility, or even hope.

    o *Example: "When you walk out of this room and back into the field, remember this—every day, you're given the chance to change lives. In the moments that matter most, you are the difference between chaos and order, fear and safety."*

THE DIFFERENCE BETWEEN A CALL TO ACTION AND AN EVOCATIVE STATEMENT

The call to action (CTA) tells the audience what to do next. It is instructional, providing them with a clear path forward, whether it is implementing a new skill, reflecting on their performance, or preparing for the next phase of their work (Goleman, 1995).

An evocative statement, on the other hand, is about why it matters. It stirs the heart and soul, offering a reminder of the emotional and ethical weight of the profession. For police officers, who often face extreme scrutiny and pressure, this emotional connection is critical. It can reinvigorate their commitment and remind them of their purpose at moments when the job feels overwhelming (LeDoux, 1996).

By pairing a strong CTA with an evocative statement, you ensure that the audience leaves not only with a clear sense of what to do next but with the emotional fuel they need to carry that action out with passion and integrity.

PRACTICAL EXAMPLES OF EVOCATIVE CLOSERS

Here are a few examples of evocative closing statements tailored for police training sessions:

- **Officer Wellness Training**: *"Your well-being is not a luxury—it's your responsibility to yourself, your family, and every person who depends on you to be at your best. Every day you take care of yourself is another day you ensure you're there for them."*
- **Leadership Training**: *"Leadership isn't about giving orders: it's about earning trust. It is not about being perfect but about being present—always ready to step up when others hesitate. Never forget: You are the leader someone else needs today."*
- **Tactical Training**: *"In the heat of the moment, it's not your badge or your gear that will guide you—it's your heart. Trust that your courage, your training, and your values will always lead you to do what's right, no matter the cost."*

EVIDENCE-BASED INSIGHTS

The connection between emotional engagement and learning outcomes has been well documented in educational psychology. Emotions, particularly those evoked during key moments of learning, help anchor new knowledge in long-term memory and influence future decision-making (Caine & Caine, 1994). For police officers, whose actions in the field are often governed by split-second decisions, tapping into these emotions during training helps ensure that the lessons imparted are remembered and acted upon with conviction.

CHAPTER 17
TIE IT ALL TOGETHER WITH A CLEAR CLOSER

"Success is not just about reaching the destination, but how you leave the path for others."
—Unknown

Delivering a clear and confident closer to a training session is crucial for leaving a lasting impact on learners. It signals the completion of the session, ensures no ambiguity, and reinforces key takeaways. When done right, a powerful closer also encourages reflection, action, and deeper engagement with the material. As an instructor, I have found that combining evidence-based strategies with personal touches can create a memorable and lasting conclusion that leaves learners inspired and eager to apply what they have learned.

WHY A CLEAR CLOSER MATTERS

The end of a session is not just a formal goodbye; it is a critical moment for cementing what was learned. Studies show that learners retain information more effectively when presented in structured formats, particularly at the beginning and end of a session. This phenomenon, known as the "serial position effect," underscores the importance of recency—the idea that people remember the last things they hear (Murdock, 1962). A confident, purposeful closer takes advantage of this, reinforcing key points while leaving a positive, lasting impression.

Additionally, a clear closer helps manage learners' expectations and brings psychological closure to the session. Without a proper conclusion, learners may leave feeling uncertain about the session's end or unclear about the next steps (Burke & Hutchins, 2007). It is important for instructors to communicate clearly and confidently when the session has ended, leaving no room for ambiguity.

MY PERSONAL APPROACH: COMBINING PROFESSIONALISM WITH PERSONAL TOUCH

In my own experience, I noticed a significant warming reaction and overwhelming positive feedback when I began using music with an uplifting tone at the end of my presentations. The moment the farewell slide appears, the atmosphere shifts as I personally say "Muchas gracias"—a casual and heartfelt expression in my native language, Spanish. Even when delivering presentations in English, which is my second language, this gesture resonates deeply with the audience. The farewell in Spanish is displayed in a prominent and intentional fancy font, adding a touch of sophistication and personal flair.

Additionally, the slide includes a QR code with my contact information, designed with deliberate attention to contrast and color distribution for a visually refreshing experience. The combination of the QR code and design choices not only adds functionality but also creates an evocative visual impact. This approach consistently leads to an astounding round of applause and ovations, which warms my heart and pushes me to continue elevating the quality of my training. Each time, I raise the bar, setting new standards for myself and for the experience I deliver to my audience.

KEY ELEMENTS OF A CLEAR CLOSER

1. **Summarize Key Points**
   At the end of any session, learners need a brief recap of the most important points. Whether you use a summary slide or a verbal rundown, the goal is to remind learners of the session's objectives and major takeaways. Research on adult learning shows that repetition, especially during a conclusion, helps reinforce memory (Mayer, 2009). A succinct, organized summary solidifies learning and prepares learners for practical application.

2. **Announce the End Explicitly**
   There should be no ambiguity about when the session is over. Saying "This concludes our session" or "We've covered everything for today" clearly signals the end, avoiding any confusion or uncertainty. Learners need clear verbal and visual cues to know the session has formally ended (Burke & Hutchins, 2007). This simple action prevents learners from feeling like there is more to come and allows them to transition out of "learning mode" with confidence.

3. **Deliver a Call to Action**
   The closer is also an opportunity to inspire action. Ask learners to apply what they have learned or engage in a reflective exercise. Research in adult education emphasizes the importance of motivating learners to immediately use new knowledge, which reinforces learning (Knowles, 1980). Whether it is completing an assignment or reflecting on a specific scenario, a call to action ensures that the learning does not stop when the session does.

4. **Inspire with a Final Thought**
   A final thought or inspirational quote can leave a lasting emotional impact. I often choose to close my sessions with a meaningful statement or reflective question, helping learners connect on a deeper level. Research on emotional engagement in learning shows that connecting learners emotionally increases retention and motivation (Immordino-Yang & Damasio, 2007). By offering a thoughtful conclusion, you help learners tie the session to their own experiences.

5. **Use a Well-Designed Farewell Slide**
   Visual elements play a significant role in the closing moments of a presentation. A well-designed farewell slide featuring a QR code for contact information not only serves a functional purpose but also enhances the overall aesthetic of the presentation. Ensuring good contrast, color harmony, and clean design makes the closer visually refreshing, leaving learners with a positive final impression of the session.

THE EVIDENCE BEHIND EFFECTIVE CLOSERS

The effectiveness of clear session closers is backed by substantial research in learning psychology. The "serial position effect" demonstrates that learners retain the last piece of information better than content delivered mid-session, so a strong and intentional closer is vital (Murdock, 1962). Additionally, adult learning theory emphasizes that learners are highly purposeful and benefit from structured, actionable takeaways (Knowles, 1980). Providing a clear call to action in the closer enhances motivation and helps learners transfer their new skills into practical application.

The success of emotional closers is further supported by studies on affective neuroscience, which show that emotional engagement significantly enhances learning outcomes (Immordino-Yang & Damasio, 2007). Music, personal touches, and thoughtful design can evoke a positive emotional response that improves retention and elevates the learning experience.

PRACTICAL TIPS FOR INSTRUCTORS

- **Plan your closer in advance.** Make sure you know what your final words will be to avoid abrupt or unclear endings.
- **Use a visual cue,** such as a conclusion slide or farewell message, to indicate that the session has ended.
- **Offer one last engagement opportunity,** such as asking learners for a key takeaway or final question to ensure active participation until the very end.
- **End confidently,** avoiding filler words or a rushed tone, so learners feel the session had a purposeful conclusion.

CONCLUSION

The closer of a training session should never be an afterthought. By delivering a clear, confident, and well-designed closer, you ensure that your learners leave with a sense of accomplishment, motivation, and clarity. By summarizing key points, delivering a call to action, and using thoughtful design elements in your slide, you can create an emotional connection that leaves a lasting impression. My experience with music, personal touches, and evocative visuals has shown that a well-executed closer not only ends the session on a high note but also sets a new standard for training excellence.

INSTRUCTOR Z'S PRO TIP: THE ESSENTIAL DIFFERENCE BETWEEN S.T.A.R.T. AND E.N.D.I.T.

Figure 8: Essential difference between S.T.A.R.T. and E.N.D.I.T. frameworks

By now, you should recognize an essential difference between the S.T.A.R.T. and E.N.D.I.T. frameworks: *flexibility* versus *structure*. While S.T.A.R.T. allows you the freedom to choose your approach—whether you lead with a story, testimonial, analogy, rhetorical question, or takeaway—E.N.D.I.T. is not designed with the same level of flexibility.

E.N.D.I.T. was intentionally crafted to be followed in a specific order. Each step flows into the next to build the most powerful and lasting effect for your closing. Altering the sequence or skipping steps can weaken the impact of your closing, reducing its effectiveness and diminishing the lasting impression on your audience.

So while you have creative leeway in crafting your opener with S.T.A.R.T., remember that for E.N.D.I.T., sticking to the order is key to maximizing the closing's effectiveness and ensuring your message continues to resonate long after the class ends.

Remember, S.T.A.R.T. sets the tone, but it is E.N.D.I.T. that seals the deal.

CHAPTER 18

S.T.A.R.T. TO E.N.D.I.T.—A SEAMLESS LEARNING EXPERIENCE

"Success is the sum of details."
—Harvey S. Firestone

Crafting a seamless learning experience requires more than just a strong opener and closer—it requires intentional design at every stage. The S.T.A.R.T. and E.N.D.I.T. frameworks serve as powerful tools to bookend a presentation, class, or speech with impact. However, it is essential to clarify that these frameworks are not meant to diminish the importance of the presentation itself—the core of any learning experience. Rather, the goal of this book is to enhance the overall experience, ensuring that learners are fully engaged from the moment they step in until the final goodbye.

BEYOND THE BOOKENDS: THE VALUE OF THE PRESENTATION

Between the S.T.A.R.T. and E.N.D.I.T. lies the heart of the learning experience—the transfer of knowledge, the elaboration of concepts, and the unfolding of crucial learning events. It is during this phase that the true educational journey takes place. To suggest that the opener and closer could somehow replace the significance of the presentation itself would be a disservice to the purpose of the actual training.

This crucial middle is where the depth of understanding is achieved, where learners wrestle with innovative ideas, reflect on their relevance, and integrate new knowledge into their existing framework. As much as S.T.A.R.T. and E.N.D.I.T. help set the stage and tie everything together, it is in the presentation that the real learning happens.

Think of it like a flight: the takeoff (S.T.A.R.T.) and landing (E.N.D.I.T.) are vital for a safe and pleasant journey, but the experience between those points—what happens during the flight—is what defines the quality of the trip. The smoothness of the ride, the level of comfort, and the service provided during the journey all contribute to how passengers feel when they finally land. Likewise, in a learning experience, the delivery of content between the opener and closer determines the depth of learning and the extent of engagement.

THE ROLE OF S.T.A.R.T. AND E.N.D.I.T.

The S.T.A.R.T. framework is designed to ensure the learning journey begins on solid ground. By using a Story, Testimonial, Analogy, or Rhetorical Question, instructors can captivate attention and set a purposeful tone for the session. When learners see relevance from the beginning, they are more likely to be engaged throughout the presentation.

On the other end, the E.N.D.I.T. framework guarantees that the session concludes with impact. By ensuring no questions remain, nailing down key takeaways, driving action, inspiring with a statement, and tying it all together, E.N.D.I.T. leaves learners with clarity and a sense of direction.

This structured ending solidifies the learning experience and empowers participants to apply what they have learned.

Yet, these bookends are not standalone. They are crafted to enhance the presentation, not replace it. The value of the S.T.A.R.T. and E.N.D.I.T. frameworks lies in their ability to make the entire session cohesive and engaging from start to finish, elevating the learning experience to a level where learners feel connected, informed, and empowered.

A COMPLETE FLIGHT EXPERIENCE

Referring to the flight analogy, S.T.A.R.T. is the smooth takeoff that ensures a confident departure, while E.N.D.I.T. is the landing that brings it all to a satisfying close. But no matter how flawless these points are, the actual flight—the middle of the journey—determines how the experience is ultimately perceived. Was the flight turbulent? Were the passengers uncomfortable? Was the service poor? Even with a great takeoff and landing, a rough middle can lead to a negative overall experience.

The same is true in learning. A seamless opener and closer can enhance the experience, but the substance delivered during the core of the presentation is where the real value lies. This is where learners connect the dots, challenge their assumptions, and absorb the insights being offered.

The objective of the S.T.A.R.T. and E.N.D.I.T. frameworks is to ensure that the entire flight, from takeoff to landing, reflects a positive and constructive learning experience. By framing the session with a strong opener and a powerful closer, these frameworks create an atmosphere where learning can thrive. However, it is the knowledge transfer during the main body of the presentation that gives the journey its substance, leaving learners with something they can take with them long after the session ends.

TRANSFORMATIONAL TRAINING: THE ULTIMATE GOAL

For over ten years, transformational training has been at the core of my presentations. From brief conference breakout sessions to week-long courses and even high-profile keynote speeches, I have built my approach around creating learning experiences that are not only informative but transformative. The S.T.A.R.T. and E.N.D.I.T. frameworks play a critical role in that process, ensuring that learners are engaged from the very beginning and leave empowered at the end.

But transformational training is about more than just the bookends. It is about what happens in between—the transfer of knowledge, the engagement with content, and the internalization of concepts that profoundly changes how participants think and act. The frameworks of S.T.A.R.T. and E.N.D.I.T. help support this, ensuring that the learning experience is smooth, seamless, and engaging from the moment learners enter the room to the moment they leave.

In closing, S.T.A.R.T. and E.N.D.I.T. are the keys to creating a complete and cohesive learning journey. They provide structure and direction, but they are never a substitute for the actual delivery of content. The entire flight experience, from takeoff to landing, needs to be carefully designed to ensure that learners leave not only with new knowledge but with the motivation and inspiration to apply it. This is the essence of transformational training—turning ordinary presentations into extraordinary learning experiences that resonate long after the session is over.

CHAPTER 19
ADVANCED STRATEGIES FOR TEACHING EXCELLENCE

> *"The best teachers are those who show you where to look, but don't tell you what to see."*
> —Alexandra K. Trenfor

In this chapter, we will explore advanced strategies for customizing the S.T.A.R.T. and E.N.D.I.T. frameworks, elevating your teaching approach from foundational excellence to mastery. These strategies are designed to help you tailor your methods to the unique needs of your audience, going beyond the basics to create truly transformational learning experiences.

1. Customizing the S.T.A.R.T. Framework for Diverse Learners

Tailor your opener to multiple learning styles to maximize engagement.

- **Advanced Tip**: Use Howard Gardner's theory of **multiple intelligences** to customize your S.T.A.R.T. framework. For example, a **visual story** works well for spatial learners, while a **testimony** from a peer can engage interpersonal learners.

Logical learners might appreciate an **analogy** that breaks down complex ideas.
- **Beyond the Basics**: Rotate the type of opener depending on your audience. For example, in a law enforcement training, use high-impact, real-world **scenarios** that create an immediate emotional and practical connection with the audience. Ask **rhetorical questions** that invite them to reflect on their own critical thinking in pressure situations.

2. Multisensory Learning in Openers and Closers

Go beyond sight and sound by engaging multiple senses.

- **Advanced Tip**: Incorporate audio, visual, and tactile elements into your openers and closers. For example, use sound effects or background music to set the tone for a story or provide interactive materials that students can manage during the analogy.
- **Beyond the Basics**: Add **kinesthetic activities** to get participants moving from the start. In a crisis intervention training, you might start with a quick group activity where students stand in different areas based on their answers to an ethical dilemma, creating both a mental and physical engagement.

3. From WIIFM to WIIFY: Personalizing the Value Proposition

Make your session about them, not just the material.

- **Advanced Tip**: Go beyond the standard "What's in it for me?" (WIIFM) and transform it into "What's in it for you?" (WIIFY). By personalizing your openers and content, you show direct relevance to each participant's specific role, challenges, and career goals.

- **Beyond the Basics**: Before class, research your audience to highlight examples relevant to their day-to-day lives. Instructors can integrate participants' real-world challenges or ambitions into the framework.

4. **Dynamic Storytelling: Evolving Narratives**

Craft narratives that grow with your audience.

- **Advanced Tip**: Instead of using a single story to introduce a session, break it into parts throughout the lesson. Start with an impactful anecdote, leave the conclusion unresolved, and return to it during key moments, making it a thread throughout your teaching. This keeps learners engaged and looking forward to each segment.
- **Beyond the Basics**: Consider using participant stories as part of the ongoing narrative. If a participant shares an insightful point during the discussion, integrate their input into the continuation of your analogy or story, making them feel like cocreators of the lesson.

5. **E.N.D.I.T. with a Call to Accountability**

End with more than action—end with accountability.

- **Advanced Tip**: Customize the call to action in your E.N.D.I.T. framework to include a level of accountability. Instead of simply asking participants to take action, challenge them to commit to a specific follow-up task and hold them accountable (e.g., submitting a plan, implementing a strategy, or presenting to their peers).
- **Beyond the Basics**: Integrate a follow-up mechanism like an accountability partner system or schedule a follow-up session

where learners must present their results from implementing the takeaways of the class.

6. Leveraging the Law of Recency and Primacy for Lasting Impact

Solidify key lessons by strategically reinforcing them.

- **Advanced Tip**: Revisit critical points strategically throughout the session using the laws of primacy and recency. These cognitive laws emphasize that learners best remember what they hear first and last, so ensure your opener foreshadows important points while your closing reinforces them.
- **Beyond the Basics**: Use **visual reinforcement** at both the start and end of the lesson. For example, begin your class with a provocative image that represents your key message and end with that same image, showing how it ties into the overall theme. This visual consistency strengthens retention.

7. Anticipatory Guidance: Preparing for Resistance

Anticipate challenges and objections and build them into your training.

- **Advanced Tip**: Build a portion of your lesson that anticipates common **resistance** or objections from learners. By acknowledging challenges in advance and offering solutions, you show respect for their expertise while demonstrating proactive problem-solving.
- **Beyond the Basics**: Use **real-time polling tools** to gauge where the resistance might lie early on, and then customize your approach to address it immediately. For example, if teaching crisis intervention, use a poll asking participants what they find most

challenging about managing mental health crises and weave their answers into your examples.

8. Active Reflection: Closing with Critical Thinking

Inspire deep reflection with powerful questions in your closers.

- **Advanced Tip**: Instead of a simple summary, use the **Inspire** element in E.N.D.I.T. to ask a reflective question that forces your learners to think critically about what they have learned. Ask open-ended questions that they can discuss or reflect on after the session ends.
- **Beyond the Basics**: Introduce a journaling activity at the end of the class, encouraging learners to jot down their reflections. Later, ask them to compare these notes to their pre-session expectations, allowing them to see how their thinking has evolved.

FINAL THOUGHTS

Going beyond the basics requires intentional design and a deep understanding of your audience. When instructors tailor the S.T.A.R.T. and E.N.D.I.T. frameworks using advanced strategies like those outlined here, they create powerful, impactful sessions that not only engage but transform learners. Remember, teaching excellence is not about following a formula—it is about constantly evolving and adapting your methods to meet the dynamic needs of your audience.

CHAPTER 20

ELEVATE AND EMPOWER— THE FINAL TAKEAWAY

"Teaching is more than imparting knowledge; it is inspiring change. Learning is more than absorbing facts; it is acquiring understanding."
—William Arthur Ward

As we reach the final pages of *The Ultimate Police Trainer's Playbook: Mastering Impactful Openers and Lasting Closers in Training*, I hope you feel equipped with the tools, frameworks, and inspiration to transform your approach to teaching and training. From the first word spoken in a classroom to the final nod of appreciation, your role as a trainer is one of profound impact. You have mastered the power of a purposeful opener, learned the art of a compelling closer, and everything in between. Now, it is time to put it all into practice.

My genuine desire for each of you is simple yet profound: to win your heart and change your mind. I have never set out to merely fill your toolkit; I have aimed to light a fire within you—to turn the good into great, to sharpen your skills, and to empower you to do the same for others. Every time you stand in front of a group, remember that transformation starts with you. Your passion, energy, and intentional design will inspire others to see new possibilities within themselves.

"As iron sharpens iron, so a man sharpens another." This timeless truth is the essence of what we have explored together. You have the ability to refine, to challenge, and to elevate not just yourself but those who will stand before you. Your journey, just like theirs, is one of constant growth fueled by the shared desire to reach new heights.

This book is not the end of your transformation; it is the launchpad. You now hold in your hands the frameworks that will not only guide your sessions but leave lasting impressions on your learners. I challenge you to use the S.T.A.R.T. framework to begin your presentations with impact and the E.N.D.I.T. framework to close them with purpose. More importantly, I challenge you to *live* these concepts—to teach not by default but by intentional design.

The future is in your hands, and your next session is your canvas. Paint it with enthusiasm, insight, and care. Stay humble yet bold and confident. Teach with empathy, for each student is on their own journey. And, above all, lead with the heart. This is the path to becoming not just a good trainer but a great one.

Now, as you prepare to close this book, take with you a renewed sense of purpose, a deeper commitment to your craft, and the knowledge that you are a force for change. Your journey in mastering impactful openers and lasting closers has just begun—and every time you teach, you are sharpening the world around you.

Here is to the next chapter of your life as a trainer: may it be filled with excellence, authenticity, and transformation.

Go forth and inspire!

ACKNOWLEDGMENTS

To my students, past and present—thank you for shaping and inspiring me more than you know. Without realizing it, each of you has contributed to my growth as a trainer. You have pushed me to refine my craft, reminding me that I am, and always will be, a lifelong learner. It is an honor to take the stage with the responsibility of helping others in their professional development, and I do so with a genuine desire to make a difference.

A heartfelt thank you to my ILEETA colleagues. Your unwavering support and mentorship have propelled me to heights I never thought possible. You have challenged and encouraged me, and I am proud to stand beside you in this profession.

To my fellow officers and command staff, thank you for always being there to support my career. Your dedication to our shared mission and your trust in my work has been invaluable.

And to my family—my rock and my biggest fans. Your love and encouragement are the foundation of everything I do. Thank you for standing with me every step of the way.

¡VAMOS POR MÁS!

—Z

REFERENCES

Books:

- Ambrose, S. A., Bridges, M. W., DiPietro, M., Lovett, M. C., & Norman, M. K. (2010). *How learning works: Seven research-based principles for smart teaching.* Jossey-Bass.
- Ariely, D. (2008). *Predictably irrational: The hidden forces that shape our decisions.* HarperCollins.
- Bandura, A. (1977). *Self-efficacy: Toward a unifying theory of behavioral change.* Psychological Review.
- Brookfield, S. D. (1987). *Developing critical thinkers: Challenging adults to explore alternative ways of thinking and acting.* Jossey-Bass.
- Brookfield, S. D. (2013). *The skillful teacher: On technique, trust, and responsiveness in the classroom.* Jossey-Bass.
- Brinkerhoff, R. O. (2005). *The success case method: Find out quickly what's working and what's not.* Berrett-Koehler Publishers.
- Caine, R. N., & Caine, G. (1994). *Making connections: Teaching and the human brain.* Addison-Wesley.
- Cialdini, R. B. (2006). *Influence: The psychology of persuasion* (Revised ed.). Harper Business.
- Covey, S. R. (1989). *The 7 habits of highly effective people: Powerful lessons in personal change.* Simon & Schuster.

- Denning, S. (2011). *The leader's guide to storytelling: Mastering the art and discipline of business narrative.* Jossey-Bass.
- Duarte, N. (2012). *Slideology: The art and science of creating great presentations.* O'Reilly Media.
- Gagne, R. M. (1985). *The conditions of learning and theory of instruction.* Holt, Rinehart, and Winston.
- Gallo, C. (2016). *The storyteller's secret: From TED speakers to business legends, why some ideas catch on and others don't.* St. Martin's Press.
- Gentner, D. (1983). Structure-mapping: A theoretical framework for analogy. *Cognitive Science, 7*(2), 155-170.
- Goleman, D. (1995). *Emotional intelligence: Why it can matter more than IQ.* Bantam Books.
- Heath, C., & Heath, D. (2007). *Made to stick: Why some ideas survive and others die.* Random House.
- Keller, J. M. (2010). *Motivational design for learning and performance: The ARCS model approach.* Springer.
- Knowles, M. S. (1980). *The modern practice of adult education: From pedagogy to andragogy.* Cambridge Adult Education.
- Knowles, M. S., Holton, E. F., & Swanson, R. A. (2015). *The adult learner: The definitive classic in adult education and human resource development* (8th ed.). Routledge.
- Kouzes, J. M., & Posner, B. Z. (2017). *The leadership challenge: How to make extraordinary things happen in organizations.* John Wiley & Sons.
- LeDoux, J. E. (1996). *The emotional brain: The mysterious underpinnings of emotional life.* Simon & Schuster.
- Marzano, R. J. (2017). *The new art and science of teaching.* Solution Tree Press.
- Mayer, R. E. (2001). *Multimedia learning.* Cambridge University Press.
- Mayer, R. E. (2009). *Multimedia learning.* Cambridge University Press.

- Mayer, R. E. (2014). *The Cambridge handbook of multimedia learning* (2nd ed.). Cambridge University Press.
- Medina, J. (2014). *Brain rules: 12 principles for surviving and thriving at work, home, and school.* Pear Press.
- Merriam, S. B., & Bierema, L. L. (2014). *Adult learning: Linking theory and practice.* Jossey-Bass.
- Noe, R. A. (2017). *Employee training and development.* McGraw-Hill Education.
- Rosenshine, B. (2012). *Principles of instruction: Research-based strategies that all teachers should know.* Jossey-Bass.
- Sousa, D. A. (2011). *How the brain learns* (4th ed.). Corwin Press.
- Sweller, J. (2011). *Cognitive load theory.* Springer.
- Willingham, D. T. (2009). *Why don't students like school? A cognitive scientist answers questions about how the mind works and what it means for the classroom.* Jossey-Bass.
- Zull, J. E. (2002). *The art of changing the brain: Enriching teaching by exploring the biology of learning.* Stylus Publishing.

Journal Articles:

- Deci, E. L., & Ryan, R. M. (2000). The "what" and "why" of goal pursuits: Human needs and the self-determination of behavior. *Psychological Inquiry, 11*(4), 227–268.
- Graesser, A. C., Olde, B. A., & Klettke, B. (2002). How does the mind construct and represent stories? In M. C. Green, J. J. Strange, & T. C. Brock (Eds.), *Narrative impact: Social and cognitive foundations* (pp. 229–262). Erlbaum.
- Hattie, J., & Timperley, H. (2007). The power of feedback. *Review of Educational Research, 77*(1), 81–112.
- Murdock, B. B. (1962). The serial position effect of free recall. *Journal of Experimental Psychology, 64*(5), 482–488.

- Sweller, J. (1988). Cognitive load during problem solving: Effects on learning. *Cognitive Science, 12*(2), 257–285.

Web Sources:

- Zak, P. J. (2014). Why your brain loves good storytelling. *Harvard Business Review*. Retrieved from https://hbr.org

ABOUT THE AUTHOR

Antonio Zarzoza, widely known as "Instructor Z," is an internationally recognized police and corrections trainer, entrepreneur, keynote speaker, and police officer with over two decades of combined law enforcement experience. He currently serves as the Training Coordinator and Lead Instructor at a premier police training center affiliated with a prestigious university in Texas, where he trains hundreds of local, state, and federal law enforcement officers year-round. He is also an expert witness in police use of force, crisis intervention, and training practices for both state and federal courts.

In addition to his law enforcement work, Antonio trains corporate trainers for Fortune 500 companies in the U.S. and Mexico, helping them apply the same principles of engagement and impact that he brings to his police training sessions. His goal is to make their programs more effective and memorable. Antonio's reputation as a transformative educator comes from his dynamic, innovative, and disruptive training methods, constantly pushing to elevate good instructors into great ones.

Antonio is a Certified Force Science Analyst and a Certified Instructor, both nationally and internationally, through the International Association of Directors of Law Enforcement Standards and Training (IADLEST). He is a member and a staff instructor with the International Law Enforcement Educators and Trainers Association (ILEETA) and has served as a contract trainer for the U.S. government, providing specialized instruction to officers in Mexico and other Latin American countries aiming for police professionalization.

As a leader in training design, Antonio has been instrumental in revamping programs for the Texas Commission on Law Enforcement. He also leads Instructor Z & Associates International, a professional organization that specializes in providing comprehensive training, consulting, and design services to police and corrections agencies both in the U.S. and internationally.

Antonio's insights on police procedures, officer safety, and training design have been featured in prominent law enforcement magazines, websites, and professional journals. His book, *Not Today: 260 Empowering Affirmations for Law Enforcement: Fostering Resilience, Courage, Wellness, and Officer Safety*, serves as a practical and motivational tool, inspiring officers to build resilience, enhance wellness, and prioritize safety in their most critical moments.

Outside his professional life, Antonio finds fulfillment in spending time with his family, indulging in books, solving word puzzles, writing, and enjoying the company of his beloved pets—three pampered Xoloitzcuintles, a very loyal German Shepherd, two cynical but affectionate cats, and a mischievously sweet pet squirrel who dashes between moments of tender curiosity and bursts of wild, untamed energy. His simple yet meaningful personal life reflects the balance and joy he seeks to instill in others.

Antonio is a sought-after keynote speaker and conference presenter on various specialized topics. For booking inquiries, contact him at z@instructor-z.com.

A TIMELESS NOTE

To Ainhoa, my beautiful granddaughter,

This is a timeless note for you from when you were a baby, a small reminder of the love and inspiration you unknowingly gave me while I wrote this book. Many times, I would sit in my cozy lounge room, typing away on my laptop, feeling tired or stuck in writer's block. Then, I'd see you standing just beyond the French doors, arms outstretched, silently asking for my attention, with a smile that could brighten any day.

I couldn't resist. I'd scoop you into my arms, and back I went to work—now typing with one hand, as the other held you close. It was a sweet struggle, balancing my focus on the book while keeping you happy and entertained. Your quick, chubby baby fingers would often reach for the keyboard, trying to type your own little story. Those moments, though sometimes challenging, were the purest joy and gave me the energy I needed to keep going.

Ainhoa, my wish for you is that you always know how much your presence meant to me. You have a way of lighting up a room and lifting spirits without even trying. I hope you never lose that ability and that you always reach for the stars with the same determination and joy you had as a baby. You are a gift, and it's your love and your spirit that helped bring this book to life.

With all my love,

Grandpa, "Wampa"

Milton Keynes UK
Ingram Content Group UK Ltd.
UKHW021437011224
451693UK00012B/1095